WALCH ◆ PUBLISHING

Daily Warm-Ups

AMERICAN

GOVERNMENT

Gretchen McNulty

Level II

The classroom teacher may reproduce materials in this book for classroom use only.
The reproduction of any part for an entire school or school system is strictly prohibited.
No part of this publication may be transmitted, stored, or recorded in any form
without written permission from the publisher.

1   2   3   4   5   6   7   8   9   10

ISBN 0-8251-5898-2

Copyright © 2006

J. Weston Walch, Publisher

P.O. Box 658 • Portland, Maine 04104-0658

www.walch.com

Printed in the United States of America

Table of Contents

The *Daily Warm-Ups* series is a wonderful way to turn extra classroom minutes into valuable learning time. The 180 quick activities—one for each day of the school year—practice social studies skills. These daily activities may be used at the very beginning of class to get students into learning mode, near the end of class to make good educational use of that transitional time, in the middle of class to shift gears between lessons—or whenever else you have minutes that now go unused.

Daily Warm-Ups are easy-to-use reproducibles—simply photocopy the day's activity and distribute it. Or make a transparency of the activity and project it on the board. You may want to use the activities for extra-credit points or as a check on the social studies skills that are built and acquired over time.

However you choose to use them, *Daily Warm-Ups* are a convenient and useful supplement to your regular lesson plans. Make every minute of your class time count!

Why Government?

One of the defining features of a civilization is that it has a government. In the space below, write a few sentences in which you explain what a government is and what it does.

1

Enlightenment Authors

The documents listed below are among the most important in political history. They all explain essential philosophical principles on which our government is based. Write the letter of the correct author from the box on the line before each document.

| a. John Locke |
| b. Baron de Montesquieu |
| c. Jean Jacques Rousseau |

___ 1. *The Spirit of the Laws*

___ 2. *The Social Contract*

___ 3. *Two Treatises of Government*

2

The Declaration of Idependence

The Declaration of Independence is one of the most important documents in American history. Decide if each statement below about the Declaration is true (**T**) or false (**F**). Write the appropriate letter on the line before each statement. Rewrite any false statements to make them true.

_____ 1. The Declaration uses language that was designed both to appeal to the English people and to inspire the American people.

_____ 2. The Declaration explains that when a government is headed by a king, it should be abolished.

_____ 3. The Declaration avoids the issue of slavery.

_____ 4. The Declaration states that governments obtain their just powers from the consent of the people who are governed.

_____ 5. The Declaration contains the Bill of Rights.

Inalienable Rights

The English Enlightenment philosopher John Locke believed that all people are born with natural rights. He focused on the rights to life, liberty, and property. In the Declaration of Independence, Thomas Jefferson wrote that people are born with inalienable rights. Jefferson focused on the rights to life, liberty, and the pursuit of happiness.

Write one or two sentences to answer each question below.

1. Define the term *inalienable*. _____

   _____

2. Why do you suppose Thomas Jefferson focused on the right to "pursuit of happiness" instead of the right to "property"?

   _____

   _____

Democracy Versus Republic

The government of the United States is a democratic republic. It includes principles of both a democracy and a republic. In a pure democracy, citizens have a direct say in decisions of government. In a republic, citizens elect representatives to make decisions for them. Think about the strengths and weaknesses of each of these systems. In the table below, list at least one strength and one weakness for each system.

	Pure Democracy	Republic
Strength		
Weakness		

The Articles of Confederation and the Constitution

The statements below describe problems in the U.S. government under the Articles of Confederation. Below each statement, explain how the U.S. Constitution solved the stated problem.

1. Congress could not call on individuals for the purpose of forming a standing army. The federal government required the states to provide military troops when needed.

2. The federal government relied on the states to contribute money for federal government use. The federal government had no means to make money.

3. Individual states often taxed goods imported from other states and foreign countries. This created competition and bad feelings between states.

4. Each state issued its own paper money. As a result, money was not uniform in value. It was difficult to determine the value of goods.

6

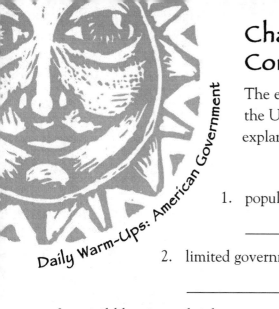

Characteristics of Early State Constitutions

The early state constitutions shared a number of traits with the U.S. Constitution. On the lines provided, write a short explanation of each concept below.

1. popular sovereignty _____

_____

2. limited government _____

_____

3. civil liberties and rights _____

_____

4. separation of powers _____

_____

5. checks and balances _____

_____

7

The Philadelphia Convention

The U.S. Constitution was developed in 1787 at the Philadelphia Convention. Decide if each statement about the Convention below is true (**T**) or false (**F**). Write the appropriate letter on the line before each statement. Rewrite any false statements to make them true.

____ 1. Delegates from all thirteen states attended the Philadelphia Convention.

____ 2. Thomas Jefferson was the primary writer of the Constitution.

____ 3. The Three-Fifths Compromise dealt with the question of how to count slaves for taxation and representation.

____ 4. The New Jersey plan proposed that representation in a national legislature should be based on population.

____ 5. Most delegates to the Convention were wealthy male landowners.

____ 6. The discussions of the Philadelphia Convention were kept secret from the public.

____ 7. Most delegates to the Convention had little political experience.

8

Confederation and Federation

When the states ratified the U.S. Constitution, they stopped using the Articles of Confederation. They went from being a confederation to a federation. In the space below, write a few sentences in which you define and compare the terms *confederation* and *federation*.

9

Purposes of the Constitution

The Preamble to the U.S. Constitution lays out the purposes of the U.S. government. Below, write a brief statement explaining the meaning of each purpose listed.

"We the People of the United States, in Order to . . .

1. form a more perfect Union,

2. establish Justice,

3. ensure domestic Tranquility,

4. provide for the common defense,

5. promote the general Welfare,

6. and secure the Blessings of Liberty to ourselves and our Posterity. . . ."

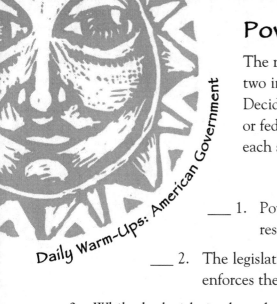

Power Divided

The national government under the U.S. Constitution is based on two important principles: separation of powers and federalism. Decide if each statement below refers to separation of powers (**S**) or federalism (**F**). Write the appropriate letter on the line before each statement.

___ 1. Powers not specifically granted to the national government are reserved for the states.

___ 2. The legislative branch creates the laws and the executive branch enforces them.

___ 3. While the legislative branch makes the laws, the judicial branch can interpret them.

___ 4. The Supremacy Clause clarifies that the U.S. Constitution is the highest law in the land.

11

Separation of Powers

The Founding Fathers wanted to make sure no one branch of the government would become too strong. To do this, they gave specific powers to each branch.

Some of these powers are listed below. Decide which branch has each power: the executive (**E**), judicial (**J**), or legislative (**L**) branch. Write the appropriate letter on the line before each power.

____ 1.   the right to declare laws unconstitutional

____ 2.   the right to declare war

____ 3.   the right to make treaties

____ 4.   the right to impeach high-ranking officials

____ 5.   the right to nominate judges

____ 6.   the right to make laws

____ 7.   the right to resolve disputes between states

12

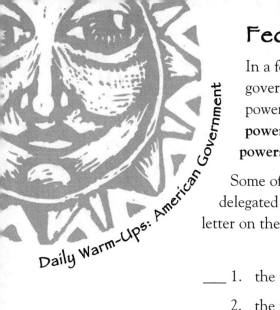

Federalism and Powers

In a federal system, power is divided between the federal government and the state governments. **Delegated powers** are powers that are entrusted to the national government. **Reserved powers** are powers entrusted to state governments. **Concurrent powers** are powers shared by national and state governments.

Some of these powers are listed below. Decide whether each power is delegated (**D**), reserved (**R**), or concurrent (**C**). Write the appropriate letter on the line before each power.

____ 1. the power to tax

____ 2. the power to coin money

____ 3. the power to conduct elections

____ 4. the power to regulate intrastate commerce

____ 5. the power to regulate interstate commerce

____ 6. the power to establish and maintain courts

13

Prohibitions on Power

The Constitution grants specific powers to national and state governments. It also prohibits national and state governments from having certain kinds of power. Decide if each statement below is true (**T**) or false (**F**). Write the appropriate letter on the line before each statement. Rewrite any false statements to make them true.

____ 1. The states can tax exports.

____ 2. The national government can tax imports.

____ 3. The national government can grant titles of nobility.

____ 4. The states can coin money.

____ 5. The states may not enter into treaties.

The Supremacy Clause

Article VI, Section 2 of the Constitution is known as the Supremacy Clause. It states:

> This Constitution, and the Laws of the United States which shall be made in Pursuance thereof; and all Treaties made, or which shall be made, under the Authority of the United States, shall be the supreme Law of the Land; and the Judges in every State shall be bound thereby, any Thing in the Constitution or Laws of any State to the Contrary notwithstanding.

In a few sentences, explain why the framers of the Constitution might have included this.

15

Federalist Founding Father: Who Am I?

I was born in the West Indies, but I was one of the Founding Fathers of the United States. I took part in the Constitutional Convention. I wrote a number of the *Federalist Papers*. I supported the creation of the First Bank of the United States. I was the first secretary of the treasury. I supported a strong national government and broad interpretation of the Necessary and Proper Clause. I was fatally wounded in a duel with Aaron Burr. Who am I?

16

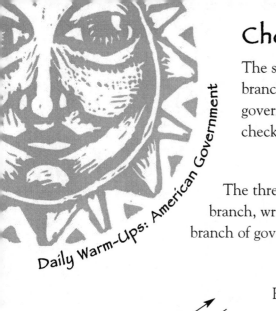

Checks and Balances

The system of **checks and balances** is the means by which each branch of government makes sure the other branches of government are doing their jobs properly. Each branch is able to check the actions of the others.

The three branches of government are shown below. Under each branch, write its major function. Next to each arrow, write how one branch of government checks the actions of another branch.

Executive

_____

Legislative

_____

Judicial

_____

17

Amending the Constitution

Article V of the Constitution explains how the Constitution can be amended. Decide if each statement about amending the Constitution below is true (**T**) or false (**F**). Write the appropriate letter on the line before each statement. Rewrite any false statements to make them true.

____ 1. An amendment can make parts of the original Constitution null and void.

____ 2. An amendment can be nullified by the Supreme Court.

____ 3. An amendment can be proposed by a two-thirds vote in each house of Congress.

____ 4. An amendment can be proposed by two thirds of the state legislatures.

____ 5. An amendment must be ratified in order to become part of the Constitution.

____ 6. An amendment must provide rights to people.

Republican Founding Father: Who Am I?

I grew up on a plantation in Virginia. I finished four years of college in two years, at what would later be known as Princeton University. I became close friends with Thomas Jefferson. I later served as his secretary of state. I was active in the Continental Congress. I took part in the Constitutional Convention in Philadelphia. I helped to draft the Constitution. I was a coauthor of the *Federalist Papers*. I was also the fourth president of the United States. Who am I?

19

© 2006 Walch Publishing

Federalists and Anti-Federalists

The Federalists were people who supported ratification of the Constitution. The Anti-Federalists were people who opposed it. Below are arguments made by the Anti-Federalists against the Constitution. Under each one, explain in your own words how the Federalists countered this concern.

1. The national government would have too much power at the expense of the states.

2. There would be no protection of the individual rights of citizens against the government.

3. Congress could do anything with the Necessary and Proper Clause.

4. The president would be similar to a king.

20

On Ambition

In #51 of the *Federalist Papers*, James Madison wrote, "If men were angels, no government would be necessary. . . . Ambition must be made to counteract ambition."

What do you think Madison meant by this? Write two or three sentences for your answer.

21

Factions

In #10 of the *Federalist Papers*, James Madison argues that the government created in the U.S. Constitution protects citizens against faction. Write one or two sentences to answer each question below about faction.

1. What is a faction?

   _____

   _____

2. How is the government structured to limit the power of factions?

   _____

   _____

3. Throughout U.S. history, has the power of factions always been limited?

   _____

   _____

22

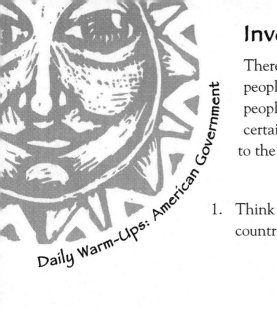

Involvement and Action

There are always policies, practices, and laws in effect that some people find inappropriate, unfair, or wrong. At the same time, people often wish there were laws to protect or provide for a certain group. Think about how this applies to you by responding to the following in the space provided.

1. Think about what you would like to change in your town, state, or country. Make a list of at least three issues that concern you.

2. Choose one item from your list above. Now make a list of at least three ways you could take action to achieve your goal.

23

American Values

What are the essential values of American democracy? Most people consider the ideals of equality, freedom, individualism, and capitalism to be important. For each term below, write a sentence or two explaining the meaning.

1. equality _____

_____

2. freedom _____

_____

3. individualism _____

_____

4. capitalism _____

_____

24

Forming Public Opinion

Newspapers and television broadcasters often talk about public opinion. They may say, "Public opinion polls show great support for the war in Iraq." Or they may say "According to public opinion, stem cell research should be opened to new cell sources." **Public opinion** refers to the general attitudes, beliefs, and ideas of a large number of people in our society about politics and other matters. Public opinion is shaped by many different factors.

Answer the following about public opinion.

1. List at least four factors or forces that influence a person's opinion.

2. Which force is the most influential? Explain your answer in two or three sentences.

25

Public Opinion Polls

We learn about public opinion through elections, media, and public opinion polls. A **public opinion poll** poses a series of questions to a portion of the population. In this way, the poll tries to identify public opinion. Poll takers then make generalizations based on the answers. Poll takers must consider the sample size, how to frame questions, how to take the poll, and how to interpret the results.

Think about all of the steps involved in taking a good poll. Now complete a short paragraph that begins with the following topic sentence:

26

Public opinion polls can be very informative, but they are not always reliable.

School Attendance

One reason you go to school is because the law requires it. In most states, laws require that anyone under the age of sixteen must attend school. These laws are evidence that our society sees a value in education.

Why do you think an educated citizenry is important for a democracy to function? Write a paragraph for your answer.

27

Common Good

The U.S. government values the rights and freedoms of each citizen. At the same time, it looks out for the common good, or the good of all people collectively. Many democracies provide extensive health and educational resources to their societies. In the United States, the role that the government takes in providing these types of resources is limited. In many cases, resources are provided by the volunteer efforts of citizens and private organizations. In fact, President George W. Bush created the White House Office of Faith-Based and Community Initiatives to support such efforts. That office offers funding and guidance to nonprofit agencies that provide services to communities all across the country.

28

Answer the following about the role of volunteers in the United States.

1. List at least three types of volunteer work or nonprofit organizations below.

2. Is it better for the government to support volunteer efforts or directly address the needs of citizens? Write at least two or three sentences for your answer.

The Media

The media plays an important role in informing and reporting public opinion. Decide if each statement about the media below is true (**T**) or false (**F**). Write the appropriate letter on the line before each statement. Rewrite any false statements to make them true.

___ 1. Media includes television news, newspapers, and news magazines only.

___ 2. Soft news focuses on human-interest stories and entertainment issues.

___ 3. All media is news, but not all news is media.

___ 4. The Internet can be a good source for hard news.

___ 5. The mass media are licensed by and overseen by the government.

29

The Roles of News Media

Choose the best answer to complete each sentence below about the news media.

1. When the news media sorts through information and decides on what stories are most important, the media is acting as a(n)
   a. watchdog.
   b. interest group.
   c. gatekeeper.
   d. advertiser.

2. When the news media investigates questionable activities of people in power, it is acting as a(n)
   a. lobbyist.   b. watchdog.   c. interest group.   d. gatekeeper.

3. The news media is supported by payments made to it by
   a. advertisers.   b. government.   c. charities.   d. politicians.

4. Under federal law, television networks are required to broadcast
   a. sports.   b. interviews.   c. documentaries.   d. news.

30

Sources and the Media

In reporting the news, journalists rely on information provided by sources. The people who provide information are not always willing to have their names shared with the general public. Sometimes sources do not want the information they share made a part of public record at all. Match each term in the box with its description below. Write the correct letter on the line.

a. on the record
b. off the record
c. not for attribution

____ 1. information given by a source in which the information may be used, but the source must remain anonymous

____ 2. information given that is confidential and meant as explanation or background; the source may not be disclosed, and information must come from a second source in order to be used

____ 3. information given by a source in which the information may be used and the source may be identified

31

Shield Laws

Most states have some kind of **shield laws,** or laws that protect journalists from having to reveal sources. Bills continue to be introduced to implement the same kinds of laws at the national level. In 2005, Judith Miller, a reporter for *The New York Times,* refused to testify before a grand jury about her sources. She was not protected by a shield law. As a result, she spent eighty-five days in jail for being in contempt of court. Later that year, Miller testified before the Senate Judiciary Committee. She said, "All are entitled to anonymity if they are telling the truth and have something of importance to say to the American people."

What does Miller mean by this? Do you agree? Write two or three sentences for your answer.

32

Interest Groups

An **interest group** is a private organization whose members work to shape public policy. An interest group can, for example, be made up of people involved in protecting the rights of animals or promoting the interests of farmers. Some interest groups focus on supporting teachers. Others advocate for the needs of older members of the population.

Answer the following in the space provided.

1. List at least four interest groups below.

2. Would you consider being a part of any interest groups? Why or why not?

33

Lobbyists

One way interest groups try to achieve their political agendas is by sending lobbyists to counsel members of Congress. Choose the best answer to complete each sentence about lobbyists below.

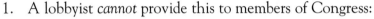

1. A lobbyist *cannot* provide this to members of Congress:
   - a. expert testimony.
   - b. background data.
   - c. literature for constituents.
   - d. vacation trips.

2. Lobbying that involves door-to-door contact, individualized e-mail, and/or regional gatherings is called
   - a. opinion polling.
   - b. grassroots campaigning.
   - c. campaigning for office.
   - d. blogging.

3. It is illegal for lobbyists to influence members of Congress through
   - a. propaganda literature.
   - b. bribery.
   - c. direct mail.
   - d. paid advertisements.

Lobbyists and Ethics

In 2005, Republican members of Congress were accused of illegally taking gifts and money from a lobbyist, Jack Abramoff. He was working on behalf of Native American tribes. This scandal caused members of Congress to propose a number of bills. These bills would require lobbyists to disclose their activities and financial dealings more fully. Other bills attempted to set limits on the contact that can take place between lobbyists and legislators. Some of the most powerful lobbyists in Washington, D.C., were dismayed by these proposals.

Write a short paragraph in which you explain what kind of contact lobbyists should be allowed to have with members of Congress.

35

Big Spenders

Lobbying groups must report their expenses at the end of each year. Some of the biggest spenders of 2005 are listed below. What issues do you think these groups spend money on? What policies do you think they hope to protect or change? Next to each name, write down one or two issues that might concern that group.

1. AARP (American Association of Retired Persons)

   _____

2. AMA (American Medical Association)

   _____

36

3. PHRMA (Pharmaceutical Research and Manufacturers of America)

   _____

4. Chamber of Commerce of the United States

   _____

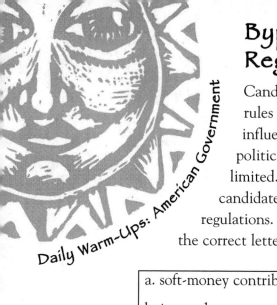

Bypassing Campaign Contribution Regulations

Candidates rely on contributions to fund their campaigns. Federal rules have tried to regulate these contributions to prevent undue influence on candidates. The amounts that individuals and political action committees can contribute to candidates are limited. Neither corporations nor labor unions can give money to candidates. There are, however, ways of getting around these regulations. Match each term in the box with its definition below. Write the correct letter on the line.

a. soft-money contributions	c. hard-money contributions
b. issue ads	d. independent ads

___ 1. money that is given directly to a candidate

___ 2. money that is given to state and local parties, not to a candidate

___ 3. ads paid for by wealthy individuals or groups

___ 4. ads that do not mention a specific candidate and are free of most regulation

37

Propaganda

Propaganda is a technique of persuasion aimed at influencing people's behavior and creating certain beliefs. There are a variety of propaganda techniques. A few of them are listed below. Define each technique in your own words.

1. celebrity testimonial _____

_____

2. personal identification _____

_____

3. bandwagon approach _____

_____

4. name-calling _____

_____

5. scare tactics _____

_____

38

Critical Consumers of Information

The public receives information from a variety of sources. These range from television to the Internet to newspapers and magazines. It is important to remember that often, the people or group compiling the information may have a particular perspective or agenda that they want to advance.

We should ask ourselves questions about every source of information to help us identify perspective and bias. In the space below, make a list of at least three of these questions.

39

Voter Behavior

People value all different kinds of things when they evaluate a political candidate. What criteria do voters consider when they select a candidate? What is important in a candidate? What do people look for in their ideal candidate? Make a list of at least five factors a voter might consider when deciding on a candidate.

40

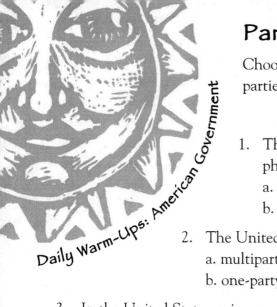

Party Lingo

Choose the best answer to complete each sentence about political parties below.

1. The formal statement of a political party's goals, agendas, and philosophies is called a
   a. coalition.
   c. platform.
   b. plurality.
   d. constituency.

2. The United States has a
   a. multiparty system.
   c. two-party system.
   b. one-party system.
   d. minor-party system.

3. In the United States, minor parties include
   a. the Democratic Party.
   c. the Independent Party.
   b. the Green Party.
   d. the Republican Party.

4. One major party working together with another major party is
   a. bipartisanship.
   c. consensus.
   b. plurality.
   d. incumbency.

41

Conservative Versus Liberal

In a political context, a conservative favors traditional views and values. A liberal is open to ideas for change and reform. Read each description below. Decide whether each is associated with a liberal view (**L**) or a conservative view (**C**). Write the appropriate letter on the line before each description. Then answer the question that follows.

___ 1. believes in strict interpretation of the Constitution

___ 2. believes in loose interpretation of the Constitution

___ 3. believes in broad interpretation of the Elastic Clause

___ 4. believes in narrow interpretation of the Elastic Clause

5. Do you think you are a liberal person or a conservative person? Why?

42

Party Types

Major and minor parties emerge in the United States and other countries for a variety of reasons. Four types of minor parties are listed below. Match each description on the left with the appropriate term on the right. (One choice will be used more than once.) Write the correct letter on the line.

___ 1. based on values

___ 2. based on conflict with a major party

___ 3. The Socialist Party is an example.

___ 4. based on the desire to reform economic policy

___ 5. based on the desire to achieve a particular goal

a. splinter parties

b. ideological parties

c. single-issue parties

d. economic protest parties

43

Why Play in the Minor Leagues?

The United States has a two-party system. As a result, it is rare that individuals in minor parties get elected to public office and have their platforms realized. Yet most political scientists agree that minor parties play an important role in American society. Write a paragraph in which you explain the importance of minor parties, using examples if possible.

44

Party Identification

The two major political parties in the United States are the Democratic Party and the Republican Party. What philosophies, goals, and issue positions do you associate with each party? Write what you know in the boxes below.

Democratic Party

Republican Party

45

Voting!

Voting is at the heart of the democratic process. Decide if each statement about voting below is true (**T**) or false (**F**). Write the appropriate letter on the line before each statement. Rewrite any false statements to make them true.

____ 1. The group of people who have the right to vote is called the franchise.

____ 2. The word *suffrage* means "the right to vote."

____ 3. When the U.S. Constitution was passed, all adult males eighteen and older could vote.

____ 4. The word *franchise* means "the right to vote."

____ 5. Women received the legal right to vote before African-American citizens received this right.

____ 6. The Thirteenth Amendment gave freed slaves the right to vote.

46

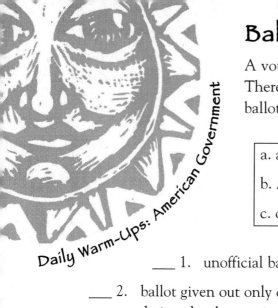

Ballots

A voter marks his or her selection in an election on a **ballot**. There are many types of ballots. Write the letter of the correct ballot from the box on the line before each description.

a. absentee ballot	d. party-column ballot
b. Australian ballot	e. sample ballot
c. office-group ballot	f. bedsheet ballot

___ 1. unofficial ballot released for public viewing prior to an election

___ 2. ballot given out only on polling day that lists all official candidates and is designed to be cast in secret

___ 3. shows candidates listed by the position for which they are running

___ 4. shows candidates listed by their political party

___ 5. ballot known for being extremely long

___ 6. ballot used for people who are not able to make it to the polling place on Election Day

47

Incumbents

An **incumbent** is someone who currently holds an office. Statistically, incumbents running for reelection have a better chance of winning than their opponents. Why do you think this is the case? Write a few sentences for your answer.

48

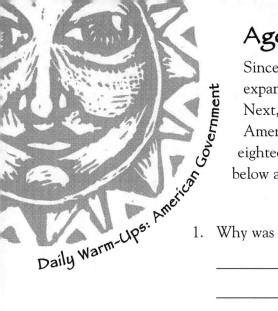

Age and Voting

Since the United States was founded, the right to vote has been expanded several times. First, it was given to African Americans. Next, it was given to women. Most recently, the Twenty-sixth Amendment lowered the minimum voting age from twenty-one to eighteen. Write one or two sentences to answer each question below about voting age.

1. Why was the voting age changed from twenty-one to eighteen?

   _____

   _____

   _____

2. Do you believe that eighteen is an appropriate voting age? Why or why not?

   _____

   _____

   _____

49

Voter Turnout

The presidential election of 2004 saw the highest voter turnout since 1968. However, just over sixty percent of eligible voters cast ballots. In a paragraph, explain why so many people in the United States do not vote.

50

Online Voting

Over the years, voting procedures have become more and more sophisticated. Online voting was first used at the state level in Arizona in 2000. What are the pros and cons of online voting? Make a list of each in the boxes below.

Pros

Cons

51

Election Day

Choose the best answer to complete each sentence about Election Day below.

1. Congressional elections are held every
   a. year.
   b. two years.
   c. four years.
   d. six years.

2. Presidential elections and congressional elections are held in
   a. November.
   b. January.
   c. October.
   d. September.

3. On Election Day, the polls close first in
   a. Oregon.
   b. Iowa.
   c. Texas.
   d. New York.

4. On any day you vote for president, you will also vote for a
   a. senator.
   b. governor.
   c. member of the House of Representatives.
   d. judge.

52

Presidential Agenda

Imagine that you are planning to run for president. What items would you put on your platform? What issues would you want to avoid?

List at least six items you want to include and six you would want to avoid. Explain why you would include or avoid each one.

Include   Avoid

53

Caucus Versus Primary Election

A caucus and a primary election are both means by which political parties determine their candidates for office. Write one or two sentences to answer each question below.

1. What is a caucus, and how does it work?

   _____

   _____

2. What is a primary election, and how does it work?

   _____

   _____

3. Which is better? Why do you think so?

   _____

   _____

54

Primary Elections

Primary elections determine which of a party's candidates will go forward in the general election for office. The two major types of primary elections are listed below. Write one or two sentences to define each type of primary. Then answer the question that follows.

1. closed primary _____

    _____

    _____

2. open primary _____

    _____

    _____

3. Which do you think is better? Why do you think so?

    _____

    _____

    _____

55

Parties and Elections

President Theodore Roosevelt once said, "An election cannot give a country a firm sense of direction if it has two or more national parties which merely have different names but are as alike in their principles and aims as two peas in the same pod." What did he mean by this? Write two or three sentences for your answer.

56

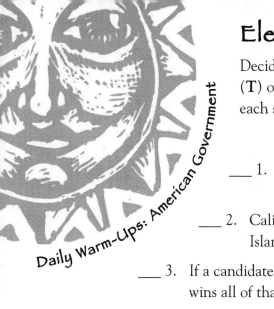

Daily Warm-Ups: American Government

Electoral College

Decide if each statement below about the electoral college is true (**T**) or false (**F**). Write the appropriate letter on the line before each statement. Rewrite any false statements to make them true.

_____ 1. A candidate can win the popular vote but lose the presidential election.

_____ 2. California has the same number of electoral votes as Rhode Island.

_____ 3. If a candidate wins fifty-three percent of the vote in New York, he or she wins all of that state's electoral votes.

_____ 4. A candidate becomes president by winning a majority of electoral votes.

_____ 5. The number of electors a state has is based on the state's congressional representation.

_____ 6. The electoral college was designed to protect the interests of small states.

57

Challenges to the Electoral College

In recent years, the electoral college system has been criticized. Opponents to the system has been criticized highlight the following issues:

- A candidate can win the presidency without winning the popular vote, as happened in the 2000 presidential election.

- Electors do not have to vote in accord with the popular vote.

- If an electoral majority is not achieved, the House of Representatives could end up choosing the president.

Are these issues reason enough to change the electoral college system? Why or why not? Explain your answer in a paragraph.

58

The House and the Senate

Decide if each description below refers to the House of Representatives (**H**) or the Senate (**S**). Write the appropriate letter on the line before each statement.

____ 1. branch in which the president *pro tempore* serves

____ 2. branch in which members serve two-year terms

____ 3. branch referred to as the "upper house"

____ 4. branch in which members are required to be at least twenty-five years old

____ 5. branch whose members have the larger constituency

____ 6. branch in which the majority of work is done in committees

59

Representation in the House of Representatives

Match each term in the box with its description below. Write the correct letter on the line. Then answer the questions that follow.

| a. gerrymandering | b. census | c. apportionment |

___ 1. an official counting of the population

___ 2. dividing a geographic region such as a state into voting districts in order to give an advantage to one political party

___ 3. the distribution of representatives among the states, based on population

4. Which states have the most seats in the House of Representatives?

5. How often does a census occur in the United States?

6. Is gerrymandering unfair? Why or why not?

60

Of Congress

In 1846, President James Polk made the statement, "There is more selfishness and less principle among members of Congress . . . than I had any conception of, before I became President of the U.S." What do you think he meant by this? Do you agree? Write a few sentences for your answer.

© 2006 Walch Publishing

Leadership in the House of Representatives

One of the reasons the House of Representatives runs smoothly is because there are clearly defined leadership roles. Write one or two sentences to answer each question below about the speaker of the House.

1. How is the speaker of the House chosen?

   _____

   _____

2. What are the speaker's major responsibilities?

   _____

   _____

3. Who is the current speaker of the House?

   _____

   _____

62

Party Leaders

Leaders of the two major political parties play an important role in Congress. They direct the conduct of business in both the House of Representatives and the Senate. Choose the best answer to complete each sentence about party leaders below.

1. The majority leader of the House of Representatives is elected by
   a. the entire House of Representatives.
   b. the entire House of Representatives and the Senate.
   c. members of the majority party in the House of Representatives.
   d. members of the majority party in the House of Representatives and the Senate.

2. The majority whip of the Senate
   a. assists the majority leader.
   b. writes legislation.
   c. keeps tabs on party members.
   d. both *a* and *c*

3. The majority leader of the House of Representatives
   a. outranks the speaker of the House.
   b. is elected by party members.
   c. is reelected every year.
   d. always comes from a large state.

63

Leadership in the Senate

Write one or two sentences to answer each question below about leadership in the Senate.

1. How is the president of the Senate determined?

   _____

   _____

2. What are the president's major responsibilities?

   _____

   _____

64

3. How is the president *pro tempore* determined? _____

   _____

4. What are the president *pro tempore*'s major responsibilities? _____

   _____

House and Senate Powers

The House of Representatives and the Senate make up the legislative branch of the U.S. government. Decide if each description below refers to the House of Representatives (**H**) or the Senate (**S**). Write the appropriate letter on the line before each statement.

___ 1. chamber in which a bill of revenue originates

___ 2. chamber in which an official can be impeached

___ 3. chamber in which an impeached official can be tried

___ 4. chamber in which the vice president can break a tie vote

___ 5. chamber that can approve presidential appointees

___ 6. chamber that has the power to ratify treaties

65

The Business of Congress

There is a great deal of jargon involving the day-to-day business of Congress. Match each term in the box with its description below. Write the correct letter on the line.

a.	*Congressional Record*	d.	session
b.	bipartisan	e.	term
c.	special session	f.	quorum

_____ 1. involving both major political parties

_____ 2. the minimum number of members who must be present in order for a vote or an action to be taken

_____ 3. the length of time a member of Congress is assigned to serve

_____ 4. the official meeting of Congress for the purpose of conducting business

_____ 5. the official transcripts (including revisions and extensions) of all proceedings in the House, the Senate, and related committees

_____ 6. a meeting of one or both houses of Congress that is scheduled outside of the official meeting time

66

Bills

Bills must originate in the House or the Senate. Yet proposed laws are seldom written by legislators. Instead, laws might be written by a Cabinet department (for instance, the Department of Transportation). Laws are also written by lobbying agencies (for instance, the American Medical Association). What are the pros and cons of this system? Write your ideas in the space below.

Pros   Cons

67

From Bill to Law

A bill is a piece of proposed legislation. Before a bill becomes a law, it undergoes a great deal of scrutiny. Decide if each statement about bills below is true (**T**) or false (**F**). Write the appropriate letter on the line before each statement. Rewrite any false statements to make them true.

___ 1. If a bill is passed by a simple majority of both the House and the Senate and is signed by the president, it becomes law.

___ 2. If a bill is passed by a simple majority of both the House and the Senate, but the president vetoes the bill, the bill still becomes a law.

___ 3. If the House and the Senate each pass a bill by a simple majority within ten days of the end of a congressional session, and the president takes no action, the bill becomes law.

___ 4. A pocket veto occurs when the president takes no action on a bill within ten days of a congressional adjournment.

___ 5. Congress can override a presidential veto with a two-thirds vote of the Senate.

68

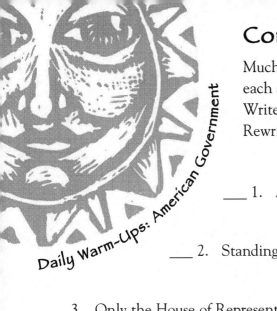

Committees of Congress

Much of the work of Congress is done in committees. Decide if each statement about committees below is true (**T**) or false (**F**). Write the appropriate letter on the line before each statement. Rewrite any false statements to make them true.

____ 1. A standing committee is permanently in existence.

____ 2. Standing committees exist only in the House of Representatives.

____ 3. Only the House of Representatives has a Budget Committee.

____ 4. Each Appropriations Committee deals with spending bills.

____ 5. The House Ways and Means Committee deals with taxation.

69

Senators and Representatives

Think about your state, the people who represent it, and the interests of the constituency. Then answer the following.

1. Name the two U.S. senators from your state.

2. Name your U.S. representative.

3. Think about the activities and interests of people in your state. On what committees would you like your U.S. senators or representatives to serve? Why? List at least two committees, and explain your reasoning in a paragraph.

70

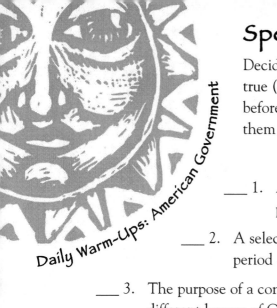

Specialized Congressional Committees

Decide if each statement about congressional committees below is true (**T**) or false (**F**). Write the appropriate letter on the line before each statement. Rewrite any false statements to make them true.

___ 1. A joint committee is made up of members of all political parties.

___ 2. A select or special committee is often created to last only for a short period of time.

___ 3. The purpose of a conference committee is to reconcile bills from the different houses of Congress.

___ 4. A conference committee is made up of members of both the House and the Senate.

___ 5. Committee chairs are chosen by members of all parties.

___ 6. The majority party gets nine tenths of the seats on each standing committee.

71

Rules

The House of Representatives and the Senate conduct business in different ways. The House, for instance, has extensive rules. In fact, bills need to go through the Rules Committee before they hit the House floor. The Senate, on the other hand, has few rules. Senators seldom place limitations on legislative debate. Why do you think the two houses of Congress operate so differently? Write two or three sentences for your answer.

72

Filibuster

The term *filibuster* refers to a stalling tactic. In a clear paragraph, explain how this technique is used, in which house of Congress it is used, and why it might be necessary.

Seniority Rule

The seniority rule is an unwritten rule. According to this rule, important positions of leadership, such as committee chairmanships, are held by those with the longest records of service in Congress.

What are the advantages and disadvantages of the seniority rule? In the space below, list at least two advantages and two disadvantages.

Advantages   Disadvantages

74

Benefits of Serving in Congress

Being a member of Congress brings many benefits. These include travel allowances, offices, a budget for hiring staff, and the ability to mail letters postage-free. (This mailing benefit is known as the franking privilege.) Members of Congress also have access to parking, free printing, restaurants, gymnasiums, and more. Do you think members of Congress deserve such privileges? Why or why not? Write your ideas in a paragraph.

75

Types of Taxes

One way government raises money is through taxation. Several different types of taxation are listed below. Match each term in the box with its description. Write the correct letter on the line.

| a. flat tax | b. regressive tax | c. progressive tax |

___ 1. A tax that takes a percentage of a person's income; as income level increases, so does the percentage of the tax.

___ 2. A tax that is based on a percentage of a person's income; the percentage stays constant at any income level.

___ 3. A tax in which the proportion of tax paid relative to income decreases as income increases.

___ 4. Sales tax is an example of this type of tax.

___ 5. Income tax is an example of this type of tax.

76

Tax Time

The most common types of taxes are listed below. Match each term in the box with its description below. Write the correct letter on the line.

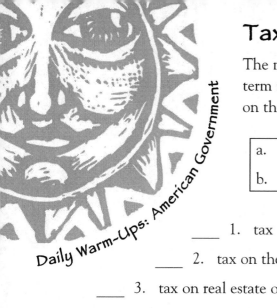

a. property tax	c. estate tax	e. inheritance tax
b. sales tax	d. income tax	f. excise tax

_____ 1. tax on a commodity, paid by the purchaser

_____ 2. tax on the earnings of an individual or a corporation

_____ 3. tax on real estate or personal possessions

_____ 4. tax on the manufacture or consumption of goods or performance of services

_____ 5. tax on the assets of a person who has died

_____ 6. tax on a beneficiary's gains from an estate

77

Taxation

Taxation occurs at all levels of government. In the chart below, list two or three types of taxes that are commonly used at each level of government. You may use some types of taxes more than once.

State Government	Township or City Government	National Government

78

Congress and Judiciary Matters

The Constitution makes certain provisions for the use of legislative power in judicial matters. It specifically addresses the following legal actions: **bill of attainder, ex post facto law,** and **writ of habeas corpus.** Fill in the appropriate term next to each definition below. Then note what the Constitution says about each in the space provided.

_____ 1. An order that requires evidence to be presented or a charge to be filed against a prisoner in order to hold him or her. The Constitution says:

_____ 2. An act that allows a person to be pronounced guilty of a crime without a trial. The Constitution says:

_____ 3. A law that punishes an offender for committing an offense prior to the law having been passed. The Constitution says:

79

Copyrights and Patents

A **copyright** is the exclusive right to reproduce, publish, and sell creative work. Copyrights are registered by the Copyright Office in the Library of Congress. A **patent** grants the exclusive right to make, use, or sell an invention. Patent laws are administered by the Patent and Trademark Office in the Department of Commerce. Briefly answer each question below about patents and copyrights.

1. Why are copyrights and patents important? _____

   _____

2. Why does the government regulate copyrights and patents? _____

   _____

3. If a pharmaceutical manufacturer develops a new, lifesaving drug, should the manufacturer be able to patent it and limit production? Why or why not?

   _____

4. Should music accessible on the Internet be protected by copyright? Why or why not?

   _____

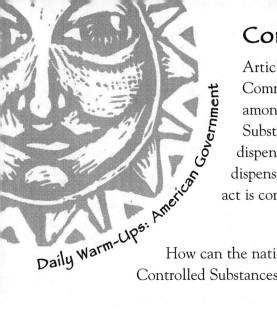

Commerce Clause and Drug Control

Article I, Section 8, Clause 3 of the Constitution is known as the Commerce Clause. It allows Congress to regulate commerce among the states. Currently, the national government's Controlled Substances Act makes it illegal "to manufacture, distribute, or dispense, or possess with intent to manufacture, distribute, or dispense, a controlled substance." The government claims that this act is constitutional under the Commerce Clause.

How can the national government use the Commerce Clause to justify the Controlled Substances Act? Write a few sentences for your answer.

81

Bankruptcy

Congress has the right to make laws involving bankruptcy. Generally speaking, bankruptcy frees a debtor from having to repay debts. Think about bankruptcy, and answer the questions below.

1. List two or three factors that could lead an individual or a corporation to file for bankruptcy.

   _____

   _____

2. Should filing for bankruptcy be allowed? Why or why not? Write a few sentences for your answer.

   _____

   _____

   _____

Daily Warm-Ups: American Government

82

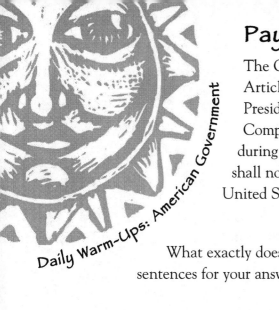

Pay Raises

The Constitution addresses the matter of the president's salary. Article II, Section 1, Clause 7 of the Constitution states, "The President shall, at stated Times, receive for his Services, a Compensation, which shall neither be increased nor diminished during the Period for which he shall have been elected, and he shall not receive within that Period any other Emolument from the United States, or any of them."

What exactly does this clause mean? Why is it important? Write a few sentences for your answer.

83

© 2006 Walch Publishing

The Necessary and Proper Clause

Article I, Section 8, Clause 18 of the Constitution states that Congress has the power "To make all Laws which shall be necessary and proper for carrying into Execution the foregoing Powers and all other Powers vested by this Constitution in the Government of the United States, or in any Department or Officer thereof." This is the Necessary and Proper Clause. It is one of the most important clauses in the Constitution. It is sometimes called the Elastic Clause, because it can be stretched to cover many situations. When interpreted strictly, it limits government powers to what is fairly explicit in the Constitution. When interpreted loosely, it can allow for the government to become expansive and

Do you think the Necessary and Proper Clause should be interpreted strictly or loosely? Why? Write a few sentences for your answer.

84

Passing a Revenue Bill

A revenue bill follows a long path from its beginnings to its passage into law. Answer the following.

1. Define *revenue bill*.

   _____

   _____

2. In order, number the stages the bill must go through to become a law. Write the correct numbers on the lines.

   ___ a. U.S. president

   ___ b. Senate Finance Committee

   ___ c. House Ways and Means Committee

   ___ d. conference committee

   ___ e. Rules Committee

   ___ f. Senate floor

   ___ g. House floor

85

Name Game

The leaders of the executive branch of the United States government are some of the most influential people in the world. Who are they? Write in the names of the individuals who currently hold the positions below.

1. President _____

2. Vice President _____

3. Secretary of State _____

4. Secretary of Defense _____

5. National Security Advisor _____

6. Homeland Security Secretary _____

7. Attorney General _____

8. Chief of Staff _____

86

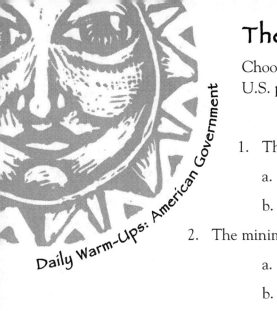

The President

Choose the best answer to complete each sentence about the U.S. president below.

1. The president serves for a term of

   a. two years.   c. six years.

   b. four years.   d. eight years.

2. The minimum age requirement for the president is

   a. twenty-five years old.   c. thirty-five years old.

   b. thirty years old.   d. forty years old.

3. The citizenship requirement for the president is

   a. five years.   c. fourteen years.

   b. ten years.   d. a lifetime.

4. The president can be impeached for

   a. treason.   c. high crimes and misdemeanors.

   b. bribery.   d. all of the above

87

Unwritten Qualifications

The Constitution outlines requirements for the U.S. president involving age and residency. However, the American voting public seems to have some unwritten requirements as well. Americans seem to want to know everything there is to know about a candidate running for president.

Write a paragraph in which you discuss some of the "unwritten" requirements for a presidential candidate. What criteria are most important to the American public? Do you agree with the validity of these criteria? Why or why not?

88

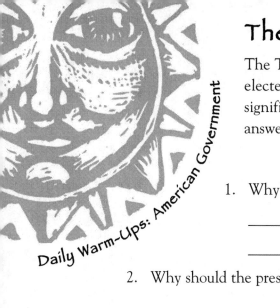

The Twenty-second Amendment

The Twenty-second Amendment states that no president shall be elected for more than two terms of office. Think about the significance of term limits. Then write one or two sentences to answer each question below.

1. Why was the Twenty-second Amendment passed?

   _____

   _____

2. Why should the presidential term be limited?

   _____

   _____

3. Should other elected offices have term limits? Explain your answer.

   _____

   _____

89

The Vice President

The U.S. president may become unable to fulfill the duties of office. In this case, the first person in line to take the position is the vice president. Write one or two sentences to answer each question below about the vice president.

1. What are the qualifications for vice president?

   _____

   _____

2. What are the two primary responsibilities of the vice president?

   _____

   _____

90

3. According to the Twenty-fifth Amendment, how is a vacancy in the office of the vice president filled?

   _____

   _____

Balancing the Ticket

Most presidential candidates choose a vice presidential candidate who can "balance the ticket." Write one or two sentences to answer each question below.

1. What does the phrase "balance the ticket" mean?

   _____

   _____

   _____

2. A candidate for president is a 49-year-old Protestant male from California. He is a graduate of Yale University who has never served in the armed forces. He is also married with no children. What type of person might this candidate choose to balance the ticket? Why?

   _____

   _____

   _____

91

© 2006 Walch Publishing

The Twenty-fifth Amendment

The Twenty-fifth Amendment explains when and how the vice president may assume the role of president. It lays out very clear protocol if the president is unable to perform duties. Either the president or the vice president and a majority of Cabinet members can inform Congress that the president is unable to carry out the duties of office. The president may resume duties by notifying Congress when no inability exists. If the president is challenged by the vice president along with a majority of the Cabinet, however, Congress decides if the president is truly fit for duty.

Why do you think the system is designed this way? Write a paragraph for your answer.

92

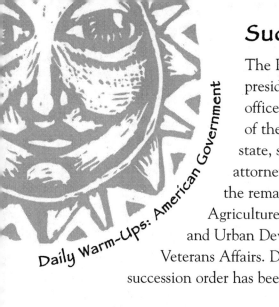

Succession

The Presidential Succession Act of 1947 says who will assume the presidency if the president dies or is unable to fulfill the duties of office. The order of succession is as follows: vice president, speaker of the House, president *pro tempore* of the Senate, secretary of state, secretary of the treasury, secretary of defense, and the attorney general. After that, the presidency would be assumed by the remaining heads of the Cabinet, in the following order: Interior, Agriculture, Commerce, Labor, Health and Human Services, Housing and Urban Development, Transportation, Energy, Education, and finally, Veterans Affairs. Debate about placing the secretary of homeland security in the succession order has been ongoing.

Think about the order of succession as described above. What is the reason for this ordering? Is there logic to it? Do you agree with this order? Write a paragraph for your answer.

93

Impeachment

Impeach means to bring formal charges against a public official. Write one or two sentences to answer each question below about impeachment.

1. What body can impeach an official? _____

   _____

2. What vote is required to impeach an official? _____

   _____

3. What body tries an impeached official? _____

   _____

4. What kind of vote is required to convict an impeached official?

   _____

5. What punishment may be given to a convicted official? _____

   _____

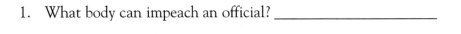

94

The President as Chief Legislator

The U.S. Constitution gives the legislative branch of the U.S. government the authority to make laws. The president does not write laws. However, the president does serve as the nation's chief legislator. What does this mean? Write two or three sentences in which you describe the president's legislative role.

95

Hail to the Chief

The president of the United States has many different duties.
Match each title in the box with its duty below. Write the correct
letter on the line.

a. chief administrator	d. chief citizen
b. chief diplomat	e. chief of state
c. chief of party	f. chief executive

_____ 1. represents the United States and its citizens when
interacting with foreign countries

_____ 2. negotiates and makes treaties with foreign countries

_____ 3. oversees and directs the many departments, offices, and agencies of
government

_____ 4. carries out the laws and dictates of the legislative branch

_____ 5. advocates for the values and agenda of his or her political affiliation

_____ 6. represents the public interests of all citizens against private interests

96

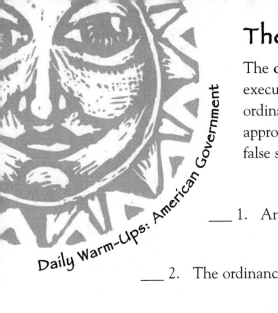

The Ordinance Power

The **ordinance power** refers to the president's power to issue executive orders. Decide if each statement about the president's ordinance power below is true (**T**) or false (**F**). Write the appropriate letter on the line before each statement. Rewrite any false statements to make them true.

___ 1. An executive order issued by the president has the effect of law.

___ 2. The ordinance power was not originally intended by the Constitution.

___ 3. The ordinance power comes from acts of Congress.

___ 4. An executive order must come directly from the president, not from any of the president's subordinates.

97

Veto Power

The president's power to use the veto is an important part of the government's system of checks and balances. Write one or two sentences to answer each question below about veto power.

1. What is a veto?

   _____

   _____

2. What is a pocket veto?

   _____

   _____

98

3. Why would a president use a pocket veto instead of a veto?

   _____

   _____

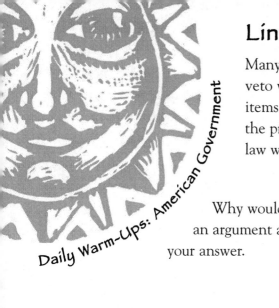

Line-Item Veto

Many presidents have called for a line-item veto. A line-item veto would give the president the power to reject individual items in a spending bill. The Line Item Veto Act of 1996 gave the president this power. However, the Supreme Court said the law was unconstitutional.

Why would the line-item veto be desirable to a president? What is an argument against the line-item veto? Write a few sentences for your answer.

99

The Budget Process

Deciding how much and where to spend money is one of the most important jobs of government. Write one or two sentences to answer each question below about the budget process.

1. What is the role of the Office of Management and Budget?

   _____

2. Who can request money from the budget? _____

   _____

3. What is the role of the president in making the budget? _____

   _____

4. How could the budget be the same from one year to the next, yet the country go from having a surplus to having a deficit?

   _____

100

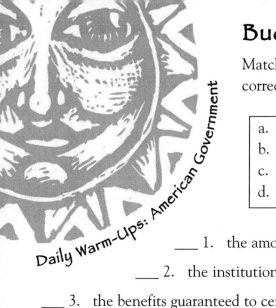

Budget Control

Match each term in the box with its definition below. Write the correct letter on the line.

a.	surplus	e.	entitlements
b.	deficit	f.	controllable spending
c.	public debt	g.	uncontrollable spending
d.	Federal Reserve System		

____ 1. the amount that the government has borrowed and needs to repay

____ 2. the institution that controls monetary policy in the United States

____ 3. the benefits guaranteed to certain groups or individuals, such as unemployment or Medicare

____ 4. the result of spending more money than is taken in

____ 5. the result of taking in more money than is spent

____ 6. spending that cannot be changed directly by the president and Congress

____ 7. amount decided upon by the president and Congress that is spent on a variety of programs

101

Balancing the Budget

The federal government has the power to practice deficit financing. This means that the government borrows money when its income is not sufficient to cover spending needs. In 1997, Congress passed a Balanced Budget Act. It barred deficit spending. The public debt was paid off, leaving the country with a small surplus by 2001. By the year 2002, however, the country saw a return to public debt.

Should the country have a balanced budget no matter what? When is it acceptable to incur public debt? Write a paragraph for your answer.

102

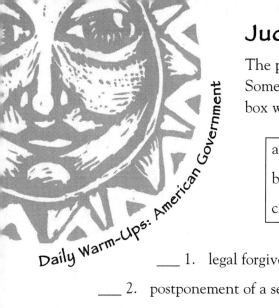

Judicial Powers of the President

The president can use certain powers to check the judicial branch. Some of these powers are listed below. Match each power in the box with its description. Write the correct letter on the line.

a. amnesty	d. conditional pardon
b. clemency	e. pardon
c. commutation	f. reprieve

___ 1. legal forgiveness of a crime offered to an individual

___ 2. postponement of a sentence

___ 3. legal forgiveness of a crime offered to a group of offenders

___ 4. legal forgiveness of a crime offered to an individual once certain stipulations have been met

___ 5. reduction in the severity of the sentence

___ 6. any act that shows mercy or leniency toward an offender

103

Presidential Appointments

The president has the power to appoint individuals to key positions in government, with the consent of the Senate. Decide if the president has the power of appointment for each position below. Write **Y** for yes or **N** for no on the line before each position. For each position that is not a presidential appointment, say how the position is achieved.

____ 1. ambassadors

____ 2. speaker of the House

____ 3. Cabinet member

____ 4. armed forces officers

____ 5. president *pro tempore* of the Senate

____ 6. state appeals judge

____ 7. federal court judge

____ 8. head of the Central Intelligence Agency

104

The Bureaucracy

A **bureaucracy** is a complex structure that takes care of the everyday business of an organization. The federal bureaucracy is no different. It consists of a hierarchy of officials. These officials have specialized jobs and follow a certain set of rules to make the government function. There are three major divisions of the federal bureaucracy. Match each division of the bureaucracy in the box with its descriptions below. Write the correct letter on the line.

> a. Executive Office of the President
>
> b. executive departments
>
> c. independent agencies

___ 1. Each one of these is headed by a member of the Cabinet.

___ 2. The National Security Council falls under this division.

___ 3. The Central Intelligence Agency falls under this division.

___ 4. The president's closest advisors come from this division.

___ 5. The Department of Homeland Security falls under this division.

___ 6. The secretary of the treasury falls under this division.

105

Serving in the Bureaucracy

Over two million people work for the federal government. Match each term in the box with its description below. Write the correct letter on the line. Then answer the question that follows.

a. civil service	c. classified service
b. patronage	d. unclassified

____ 1. giving jobs to friends or supporters

____ 2. government positions that are based on merit or quality of work and require examinations

____ 3. civilian employees of the federal government

____ 4. government positions that do not require examinations

5. Is the practice of patronage fair? Why or why not? Write one or two sentences for your answer.

106

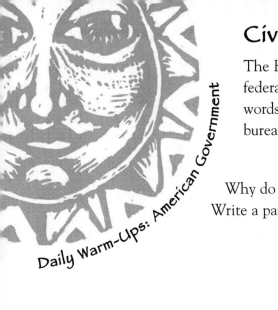

Civil Servants and Politics

The Hatch Act of 1939, and its 1993 amendments, prohibit federal employees from running in partisan elections. In other words, they cannot hold public office while they are part of the bureaucracy.

Why do you think this is the case? Is this fair? Why or why not? Write a paragraph for your answer.

107

The Imperial Presidency

In recent years, the job of the U.S. president has sometimes been referred to as the imperial presidency. Write one or two sentences to answer each question below about the power of the president.

1. What does the word *imperial* mean? _____

   _____

   _____

2. Is the term *imperial presidency* a criticism? Why or why not?

   _____

   _____

3. How has the power of the president grown since the country began?

   _____

   _____

108

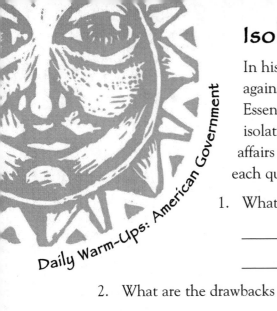

Isolationism

In his farewell address, President George Washington advised against making close friends or enemies of other nations. Essentially, he was suggesting a foreign policy based on isolationism. **Isolationism** involves separating oneself from the affairs of other countries. Write one or two sentences to answer each question below about isolationism.

1. What are the benefits of isolationism?

   _____

   _____

2. What are the drawbacks of isolationism?

   _____

   _____

3. Is it possible today for the United States to remain isolated from other countries? Why or why not?

   _____

   _____

109

Interventionism

Interventionism refers to taking an active role in the affairs of other countries. Write one or two sentences to answer each question below about interventionism.

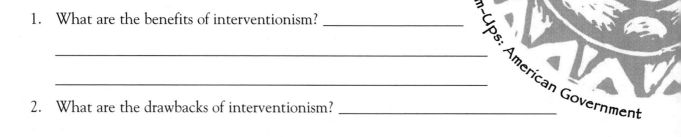

1. What are the benefits of interventionism? _____

_____

_____

2. What are the drawbacks of interventionism? _____

_____

_____

3. When is interventionism important or justified? Explain your answer.

_____

_____

110

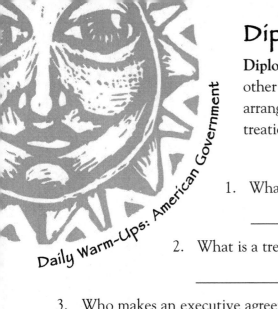

Diplomacy and Foreign Policy

Diplomacy involves making arrangements and agreements with other countries. The United States has two ways of making formal arrangements with other countries: executive agreements and treaties. Answer each question below about diplomacy.

1. What is an executive agreement? _____ _____

2. What is a treaty? _____ _____

3. Who makes an executive agreement? _____

4. Who makes a treaty?_____

5. Who must approve an executive agreement? _____

6. Who must approve a treaty? _____

111

War Powers

As commander in chief of the nation's armed forces, the president has the power to deploy troops and authorize missions. This power is "checked" by the extensive powers held by Congress. Answer the following about war powers.

1. List at least three legislative powers regarding international conflict.

112

2. In the War Powers Resolution of 1973, Congress authorized itself to limit the use of troops in nonwar zones. Why did it do this? Write two or three sentences for your answer.

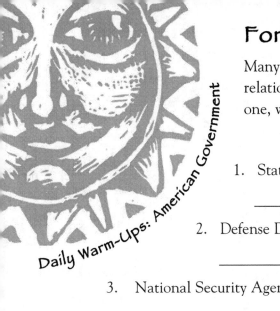

Foreign Relations

Many different U.S. departments and agencies deal with foreign relations. Some of these organizations are listed below. For each one, write one or two sentences explaining its role.

1. State Department _____

   _____

2. Defense Department _____

   _____

3. National Security Agency _____

   _____

4. Joint Chiefs of Staff _____

   _____

113

The Right of Legation

The right of legation is the right of a country to conduct diplomatic relations. **Ambassadors** are the official representatives of the United States in foreign countries. A U.S. ambassador and a staff of diplomatic representatives, called an embassy, can be found in over 180 countries around the world.

What are the responsibilities and objectives of an ambassador? Write a paragraph for your answer.

114

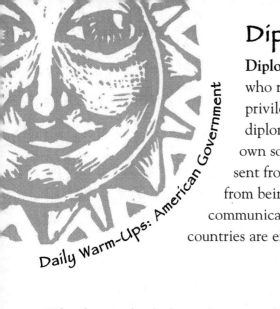

Diplomatic Immunity

Diplomatic immunity refers to special privileges given to those who represent another country in the United States. These privileges include freedom from arrest, search, and taxation. The diplomat of another country is considered to be on that country's own soil, even when he or she is in the United States. Anything sent from the diplomat back to his or her home country is exempt from being seized or searched. A diplomat's residence and communications are protected as well. U.S. diplomats in foreign countries are extended the same privilege.

Why do you think this policy is in place? Do you agree with this practice? Why or why not? Write a paragraph for your answer.

115

The Armed Forces

In the table below, list the three main departments of the nation's armed forces. Describe each department's responsibility. Then answer the question that follows.

Division	Responsibility
1.	
2.	
3.	

116

4. Are there other armed forces that protect our country? List as many as you can think of.

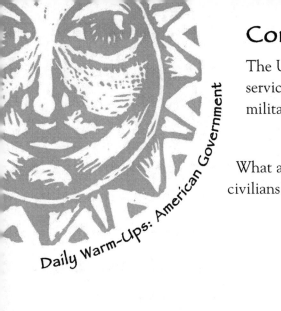

Control of the Armed Services

The U.S. Constitution provides for civilian control of the armed services. The president and the secretary of defense are both non-military.

What are the benefits and drawbacks of a military controlled by civilians? Write a paragraph for your answer.

117

The Draft

All males who are eighteen years old are required to register for the draft, also known as conscription. The armed forces are able to conduct affairs through voluntary service. This registration, though, currently allows the government to identify young men who could be ordered into military service if needed. (Actually putting the draft back into effect would require approval by Congress.) Write one or two sentences to answer each question below about the draft.

1. In what instances do you think a draft is appropriate?

   _____

   _____

118

2. Should women have to register for the draft? Why or why not?

   _____

   _____

Supreme Court Membership

The most powerful court in the country is the U.S. Supreme Court. Write one or two sentences to answer each question below about the Supreme Court.

1. How many judges are there on the Supreme Court?

   _____

2. How old does a person have to be in order to be nominated for the Supreme Court?

   _____

3. What kind of background or experience does a person need in order to be on the Supreme Court?

   _____

4. Do you think there should be additional criteria for Supreme Court nominees? Why or why not?

   _____

   _____

119

Who Is on the Supreme Court?

The Supreme Court is made up of the Chief Justice of the United States and eight associate judges. It is the final authority in all questions of federal law.

Answer the following about the Supreme Court.

1. Name the Chief Justice of the Supreme Court.

   _____

2. Name the other eight members of the Supreme Court.

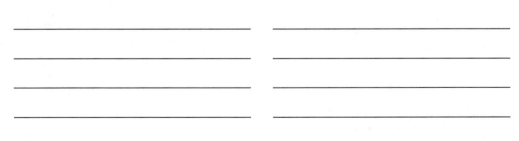

120

Lifetime Appointment

Federal court judges in both the Supreme Court and inferior courts are appointed for life. This provision was written into the U.S. Constitution. The Founding Fathers evidently considered it important.

Write a paragraph explaining why lifetime appointment for federal court judges is important.

121

Jurisdiction

Jurisdiction refers to the authority of a particular court to hear particular cases. The two major types of jurisdiction are original jurisdiction and appellate jurisdiction. Answer each question below about jurisdiction.

1. What is original jurisdiction? _____

_____

2. What is appellate jurisdiction? _____

_____

3. Does the Supreme Court hear more original jurisdiction or appellate jurisdiction cases?

_____

4. In what types of matters does the Supreme Court have original jurisdiction?

_____

122

Judicial Review

One of the weightiest powers of the Supreme Court is that of judicial review. Explain the meaning of judicial review in a few sentences.

123

© 2006 Walch Publishing

Supreme Court Case Selection

Read the paragraph below about how the Supreme Court selects cases. Then define each of the underlined terms.

Thousands of cases are appealed to the Supreme Court each year. However, the Supreme Court justices only review a few hundred of these cases. Many of those cases are <u>remanded</u> to the lower courts for reconsideration. Some cases are brought to the attention of the Supreme Court by <u>certificate</u>. However, most cases that the Supreme Court decides to hear reach the Court by <u>writ of certiorari</u>. Either party in a case can ask the Supreme Court to issue a writ of certiorari. If this is denied, the ruling of the lower court stands. Usually, the Supreme Court agrees to hear fewer than one hundred cases each year.

124

1. remanded _____

2. certificate _____

3. writ of certiorari _____

Supreme Court Trial

Read the paragraph below about how the Supreme Court tries cases. Then define each of the underlined terms.

Before they hear either side's oral arguments, members of the Court read briefs from both sides. These are documents that present information and arguments. Justices may also read *amicus curiae* briefs. The Court then hears oral arguments. These arguments are usually limited to thirty minutes per side. The justices often interrupt to ask questions. The justices then confer about the case and write opinions, often taking several months. These opinions establish precedent to guide future court proceedings.

125

1. *amicus curiae* briefs _____

2. opinions _____

3. precedent _____

© 2006 Walch Publishing

Opinions

Once the Supreme Court has heard a case, members of the Court write opinions, or their findings on the case. Three types of opinions are listed below. Explain the meaning and purpose of each opinion on the lines provided.

1. majority opinion _____

   _____

   _____

2. concurring opinion _____

   _____

   _____

126

3. dissenting opinion _____

   _____

   _____

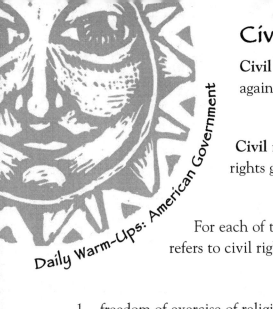

Civil Liberties and Civil Rights

Civil liberties protect individuals, their ideas, and their property against the power of government.

Civil rights are the positive acts of government that make the rights guaranteed by the Constitution available for all people.

For each of the following, write **L** if it refers to civil liberties or **R** if it refers to civil rights.

_____ 1. freedom of exercise of religion

_____ 2. protection against discrimination based on race

_____ 3. freedom of speech and press

_____ 4. protection against discrimination based on sex

_____ 5. guarantee of a fair trial

127

Bill of Rights

For the average citizen, the Bill of Rights may be the most important part of the Constitution. Answer the following about the Bill of Rights.

1. What is the Bill of Rights?

   _____

2. Where can these rights be found? _____

3. List as many of these rights as you can.

   _____

   _____

   _____

   _____

128

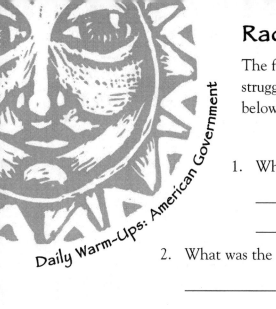

Racial Disparity

The fight for rights for African Americans was a long, slow struggle. Write one or two sentences to answer each question below about race and rights.

1. What were Jim Crow laws?

   _____

   _____

2. What was the reasoning behind the principle of separate but equal?

   _____

   _____

3. What is de jure segregation? _____

   _____

4. What is de facto segregation? _____

   _____

129

Civil Rights for Black Americans— Court Cases

Some important court cases are named in the box. Match each case with its description. Write the correct letter on the line.

> a. *Regents of the University of California v. Bakke*
>
> b. *Plessy v. Ferguson*
>
> c. *Dred Scott v. Sanford*
>
> d. *Brown v. Board of Education of Topeka*

____ 1. This 1897 case declared that racial segregation was constitutional as long as "equal" facilities were provided.

____ 2. This 1952 case determined that separate could not be equal.

____ 3. This 1978 case determined that a program could not use a race-based quota system for admission. However, a program could consider race as a factor in choosing a diverse student body.

____ 4. This 1857 case determined that Congress could not abolish slavery in the territories. It also ruled that African Americans were not U.S. citizens, therefore they could not sue in federal court.

130

Voting Restrictions

The Fourteenth Amendment to the Constitution says that no U.S. citizen can be deprived of rights without due process of law. The Fifteenth Amendment says that a person's right to vote cannot be denied or limited based on race or color. Despite this, many states found ways to limit voting rights for blacks. Some of these practices are listed below. Explain what each practice was and how it was used to limit the voting rights of African Americans.

1. poll tax _____

_____

2. literacy test _____

_____

3. gerrymandering _____

_____

4. white primaries _____

_____

131

Civil Rights and the Constitution

The fight for civil rights for black Americans involved a number of important changes to the U.S. Constitution. Match each amendment in the box with its description below. Write the number of the amendment on the line.

Thirteenth Amendment	Fifteenth Amendment
Fourteenth Amendment	Twenty-fourth Amendment

____ 1. declared "Neither slavery nor involuntary servitude . . . shall exist within the United States."

____ 2. declared that the right to vote could not be denied "by reason of failure to pay any poll tax or other tax"

____ 3. declared that "all persons born or naturalized in the United States . . . are citizens of the United States . . ." and "No State shall make or enforce any law which shall abridge the privileges or immunities of citizens of the United States . . ."

____ 4. declared that the right to vote could not be denied "on account of race, color, or previous condition of servitude"

132

Glass Ceiling

The expression "glass ceiling" has been used to describe the invisible barrier that keeps minorities from reaching the top in their careers.

What do you think accounts for such a "ceiling"? What role do you think government should play in addressing the problem? Write a paragraph in which you answer these questions.

133

Affirmative Action

Laws were passed to make discrimination illegal. But some leaders realized that minorities were still being affected by past discrimination. Many African Americans had been denied a good education. As a result, they could not get good jobs. Minorities were underrepresented in universities and in some careers.

One result of this awareness was **affirmative action**—actions aimed at improving this state of affairs. Affirmative action took various forms. Some programs only required making sure job openings were widely advertised. Others required employers to keep a certain number of jobs for members of minority groups.

134

Opponents of affirmative action claimed that these programs were reverse discrimination. They said such policies violated the rights of nonminorities.

Think about both sides of this issue. Then write a paragraph evaluating the fairness or constitutionality of affirmative action.

Free Expression

The First Amendment to the U.S. Constitution protects the right to free speech and a free press. One exception is speech that is harmful or threatening. Some types of harmful speech are listed below. Write one or two sentences to define each one.

1. libel _____

    _____

    _____

2. slander _____

    _____

    _____

3. seditious speech _____

    _____

    _____

135

The Obscenity Test

One of the gray areas involving free speech and free press involves obscenity. In *Miller* v. *California* (1973), the Supreme Court laid out a three-part test to determine obscenity. The following three questions are applied to materials in question:

1. Would the average person find that it tends to excite lust?

2. Does it depict in an offensive way sexual conduct that is specifically dealt with in an antiobscenity law?

3. Does it lack any real literary, artistic, political, or scientific value?

Think about these questions. Then write a paragraph in which you evaluate the fairness and effectiveness of this test.

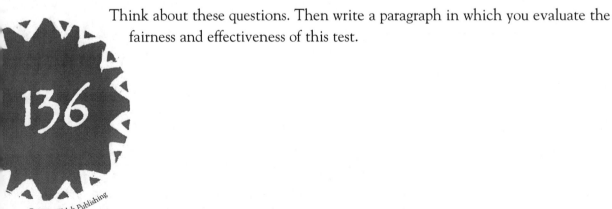

136

Religion

The First Amendment says, "Congress shall make no law respecting an establishment of religion or prohibiting the free exercise thereof." The Fourteenth Amendment supports this by saying, "No State shall make or enforce any law which shall abridge the privileges or immunities of citizens of the United States." There is a fine balance between the government allowing people to freely exercise their right to practice religion and the government supporting or establishing certain religious practices. Some of the issues raised by this balance are listed below. If you were on the Supreme Court, how would you respond to the following questions? Write one or two sentences to answer each question.

1. Should the "under God" part of the Pledge of Allegiance be changed?

2. Should students be allowed to wear yarmulkes (Jewish skullcaps) or veils (Christian or Muslim head coverings) in school?

3. Should schools be required to teach creationism in addition to evolution?

4. Should nativity scenes be allowed on public lawns?

137

Freedom of Assembly and Petition

The First Amendment to the U.S. Constitution guarantees "the right of the people peaceably to assemble, and to petition the Government for a redress of grievances." Think about this right. Then write one or two sentences to answer each question below.

1. What does *petition* mean in this context? _____

   _____

2. Why is it important that people be able to assemble freely?

   _____

   _____

138

3. What is freedom of association? _____

   _____

4. How does freedom of association relate to freedom of assembly?

   _____

   _____

Due Process Clause

Section 1 of the Fourteenth Amendment to the U.S. Constitution is also known as the Due Process Clause. It states that no state shall "deprive any person of life, liberty, or property, without due process of law."

Suppose you were accused of a crime and faced the prospect of a large fine or going to jail. What "process" would you expect to take place? Write a paragraph that explains the meaning of "due process of law."

139

Rights of the Accused

The rights of someone accused of a crime have expanded and become clearer over time. Match each term in the box with its definition below. Write the correct letter on the line.

a. exclusionary rule	d. probable cause
b. Miranda Rule	e. search warrant
c. police power	f. writ of habeas corpus

___ 1. a court order that requires the agency holding a prisoner to give the court a good reason why the prisoner should not be let go

___ 2. the right of each state to protect the safety, health, and welfare of its citizens

___ 3. reasonable suspicion that a crime has been committed

___ 4. court order authorizing the search of a specific property

___ 5. policy by which evidence gained through illegal search cannot be used against the accused

___ 6. policy requiring police to tell a suspect about his or her constitutional rights before asking the suspect any questions

140

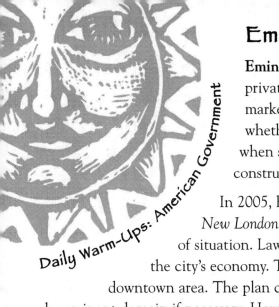

Eminent Domain

Eminent domain is a policy that allows the government to buy private property for public use. The government must pay the fair market value for the property. But it can force the owners to sell, whether they want to or not. Eminent domain is most often used when state or local governments build or expand highways, construct bridges, build dams, and so forth.

In 2005, however, the U.S. Supreme Court ruled in *Kelo* v. *City of New London* that eminent domain could also be used in a different type of situation. Lawmakers in New London, Connecticut, wanted to improve the city's economy. To do this, they approved a plan to expand part of the downtown area. The plan called for buying some property from private owners, by eminent domain if necessary. However, this property would then be controlled by a private company. Property owners protested that this was not a legitimate use of eminent domain. The Supreme Court disagreed and ruled in New London's favor.

Which side of this issue would you have supported? Write a paragraph explaining your position. Consider whether promoting economic development is justifiable grounds for eminent domain.

141

Privacy Rights

The right to privacy is not explicitly protected by the U.S. Constitution. However, in *Stanley v. Georgia* (1969), the Supreme Court noted that people have "the right to be free, except in very limited circumstances, from unwanted government intrusions into one's privacy."

The right to privacy is essentially protected by the right to due process. However, at times, the government has claimed that national security can outweigh the individual's right to privacy. This can be seen in the recent passage of laws regarding baggage inspection in airports, wiretapping, and access to e-mail.

142

Should people be willing to give up privacy in favor of security? Write a paragraph explaining your opinion.

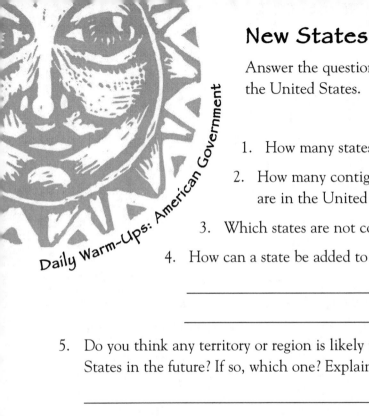

Daily Warm-Ups: American Government

New States

Answer the questions below about the individual states that form the United States.

1. How many states are in the United States? _____

2. How many contiguous (sharing boundaries, neighboring) states are in the United States? _____

3. Which states are not contiguous? _____

4. How can a state be added to the United States? _____

_____

_____

5. Do you think any territory or region is likely to become part of the United States in the future? If so, which one? Explain.

_____

_____

_____

143

Rights of Citizens in the Various States

U.S. citizens have the right to travel, buy property, do business, and settle in any state. These rights are protected by the Privileges and Immunities Clause of the Constitution. This clause reads, "The Citizens of each State shall be entitled to all Privileges and Immunities of Citizens in the several States." (This is Article IV, Section 2, Clause 1.)

States can require residency for some things. People might have to be state residents in order to receive certain types of licenses (from hunting to driving to medical practice). Only state residents might be able to pay lower tuition costs at public universities. But states cannot favor in-state residents in hiring practices or legislation involving welfare benefits.

Do you think this is reasonable? Why or why not? Write a paragraph explaining your opinion.

144

Relations Between the States

States work together in a variety of ways. Two of these ways are listed below. Explain the meaning of each term, and give an example of how it might work.

1. interstate compact _____

_____

_____

_____

2. extradition _____

_____

_____

_____

145

© 2006 Walch Publishing

Full Faith and Credit

According to the Constitution, "Full Faith and Credit shall be given in each State to the public Acts, Records, and judicial Proceedings of every other State." Based on this clause, decide if each statement below is true (**T**) or false (**F**). Write the appropriate letter on the line before each statement. Rewrite any false statements to make them true.

____ 1. If a couple gets married in Las Vegas, the marriage must be recognized in South Carolina.

____ 2. A man is driving at 65 miles per hour on the highway in Louisiana in a 65-miles-per-hour zone. When he crosses the border into Texas, where the speed limit is 55, it is legal for him to continue driving 65 miles per hour.

____ 3. A court in Connecticut has ordered a woman to pay damages in a lawsuit. The woman then moves to New Jersey. If it is asked to do so, the New Jersey legal system will enforce the Connecticut court ruling.

____ 4. A person commits a crime in North Dakota and flees to Illinois. The Illinois legal system can try and convict that person in Illinois.

146

© 2006 Walch Publishing

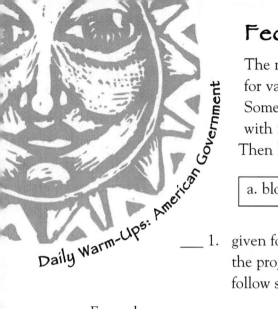

Federal Funding for States

The national government provides money to state governments for various purposes. Some of these funds are called **grants-in-aid.** Some types of grants-in-aid are listed in the box. Match each one with its description below. Write the correct letter on the line. Then list examples of each.

a. block grant	b. categorical grant	c. project grant

___ 1. given for a specific purpose; requires the state to contribute funds to the project, to provide an agency to administer the funds, and to follow specific guidelines for the use of the money

Examples: _____

___ 2. given for a specific project or service; usually provides funding for a fixed or known period; can be made to a state, a locality, or a private agency

Examples: _____

___ 3. given for a broad area of need; has few specific requirements and may be used as the state deems appropriate

Examples: _____

147

Revenue Sharing

Another type of funding to states is called **revenue sharing.** This gave states and local governments an annual share of federal tax revenues. The only restriction was that the money could not be used for programs in which discrimination was present.

Revenue sharing was common in the 1970s and 1980s. However, it is rarely seen today. In part, this is because Congress no longer supports this approach.

Why might revenue sharing have been popular with state governments, but unpopular with the national government? Write two or three sentences for your answer.

148

Power to the People!

Some states support practices that give citizens direct input into the law-making process.

Two of these practices are named below. For each one, write a sentence or two explaining the practice. If possible, name a referendum or a citizen's initiative that has been presented to voters in your state.

1. referendum _____

_____

_____

2. initiative _____

_____

_____

149

Recall

What happens if the people of a state think their governor is doing a bad job? In every state except Oregon, a governor may be removed by impeachment. In most states, this means that the state legislature can accuse, try, and remove from office an official suspected of serious wrongdoing.

Eighteen states (including Oregon) also have another mechanism for removing a governor from office. This is the process of **recall.** This is a petition procedure that relies on the voters rather than the state legislature. If a certain number of qualified voters sign recall petitions, a special election must be held. In that election, voters decide whether to keep the governor in office or choose a new governor. Unlike impeachment, recall does not require proof of wrongdoing.

What do you think are the advantages of the recall process? What are the disadvantages? Write a paragraph that evaluates the pros and cons of recall.

150

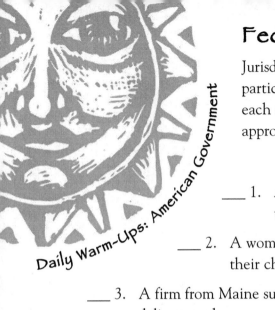

Federal and State Jurisdiction

Jurisdiction refers to the authority of a particular court to hear particular cases. Decide which court would have jurisdiction in each scenario below, federal court (**F**) or state court (**S**). Write the appropriate letter on the line before each scenario.

___ 1. A Massachusetts woman sues a man from Nevada for failure to uphold a purchase agreement.

___ 2. A woman from New York sues her ex-husband for custody of their child.

___ 3. A firm from Maine sues a Canadian shipping company for failure to deliver goods.

___ 4. A tugboat company sues another tugboat company in Virginia over the right to escort ships through a particular channel.

___ 5. The state of Montana sues a contractor for failure to fulfill a building contract.

___ 6. A company in Alaska sues a local travel agent for overcharging on airfare to other states.

151

And Justice for All

Match each court-related term in the box with its description below. Write the correct letter on the line.

a. acquittal	d. defendant
b. civil law	e. jury
c. criminal law	f. plaintiff

___ 1. in civil law, the party who files a suit or makes an accusation

___ 2. the person accused of something

___ 3. a group of citizens chosen to listen to the facts of a particular court case and decide if the defendant is guilty or innocent of the crime

___ 4. the portion of law that defines crimes and provides for their punishment

___ 5. being found not guilty of a charge

___ 6. the portion of law that has to do with relations between individuals, or between individuals and corporations or the government, not involving criminal conduct

152

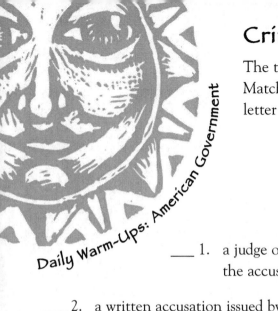

Crime and Punishment

The terms in the box have to do with crime and punishment. Match each term with its description below. Write the correct letter on the line.

a. bail	d. indictment
b. capital punishment	e. sentence
c. conviction	f. verdict

____ 1. a judge or jury's determination of the guilt or innocence of the accused

____ 2. a written accusation issued by a grand jury charging that a person has committed a specific crime

____ 3. a sum of money the accused may be required to deposit with the court to guarantee that he or she will appear in court at the proper time

____ 4. in a criminal case, the determination that the defendant is guilty

____ 5. the death penalty

____ 6. the punishment given to a person who has been convicted of a crime

153

Jury Selection

The Sixth Amendment to the U.S. Constitution promises an accused person the "right to a speedy and public trial, by an impartial jury."

What constitutes an impartial jury? Write a paragraph explaining the characteristics of a good jury.

Daily Warm–Ups: American Government

154

Justice and the Armed Services

When members of the armed services are accused of violating military law, they appear before a court-martial. This is a special military court. All court personnel are members of the armed services.

These military courts are not part of the federal court system. However, serious court-martial convictions are reviewed by the U.S. Court of Appeals for the Armed Forces. It is part of the judicial branch and is separate from the armed services.

Why is the process of trying members of the armed services set up this way? Is this system fair? Write a paragraph in which you answer these two questions.

155

State Officials

The titles of some important state officials are given below. For each one, write a sentence or two that describes that person's role and responsibilities.

1. governor _____

_____

2. lieutenant governor _____

_____

3. secretary of state _____

_____

4. treasurer _____

_____

5. attorney general _____

_____

156

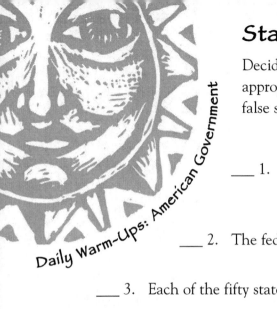

State Government

Decide if each statement below is true (**T**) or false (**F**). Write the appropriate letter on the line before each statement. Rewrite any false statements to make them true.

_____ 1. In most states, the lieutenant governor is officially the president of the Senate.

_____ 2. The federal government establishes the qualifications for governors.

_____ 3. Each of the fifty states has a written constitution.

_____ 4. Most states have a bicameral legislature with the Senate as the upper house.

_____ 5. The legislature is chosen by popular vote in every state.

_____ 6. In state governments, bills can only be introduced by the Senate.

157

State Court Law

State courts apply several different types of law. Four of these types of law are listed in the box. Match each one with its description below. Write the correct letter on the line.

a. administrative law	c. constitutional law
b. common law	d. statutory law

___ 1. unwritten law, developed over centuries from generally accepted ideas of right or wrong, applied in cases when it does not conflict with written law

___ 2. highest form of law in the United States, based on the U.S. Constitution and state constitutions

___ 3. the body of laws enacted by state or federal legislatures

___ 4. law based on rules and regulations of local, state, and federal executive offices

158

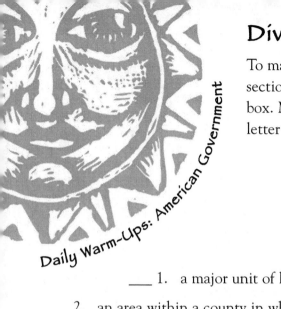

Divisions of the States

To make local governing easier, all states are divided into smaller sections. Some terms relating to these divisions are listed in the box. Match each one with its description below. Write the correct letter on the line.

a. borough	d. special district
b. county	e. township
c. parish	

____ 1.   a major unit of local government in most states

____ 2.   an area within a county in which a government is set up to perform a specific function, such as providing police protection, building bridges, or providing waste disposal

____ 3.   the major unit of local government in Louisiana

____ 4.   the major unit of local government in Alaska

____ 5.   a subdivision of a county found in about half the states

159

Education

One important function of state and local government is providing public education. Most public primary and secondary schools are paid for by property taxes. This approach has both advantages and disadvantages. List as many of both as you can.

Advantages

_____

_____

_____

_____

Disadvantages

_____

_____

_____

_____

160

Daily Warm-Ups: American Government

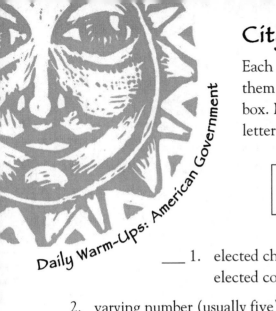

City Government

Each city has its own distinctive government. However, most of them follow one of the basic forms of government listed in the box. Match each one with its description below. Write the correct letter on the line.

a. strong mayor-council	c. commission
b. weak mayor-council	d. council-manager

___ 1. elected chief executive appoints department heads, prepares budget; elected council acts as legislative body

___ 2. varying number (usually five) of elected representatives control executive and legislative functions

___ 3. relatively weak elected chief executive, strong elected legislative body that names a chief administrative officer

___ 4. elected chief executive shares executive duties with other elected officials, including members of elected council

161

The State

There are more than 190 states in the world today, from Afghanistan to Zimbabwe.

Write a paragraph in which you explain, in your own words, what a state is. Be sure to address the topics of territory, sovereignty, and government in your paragraph.

162

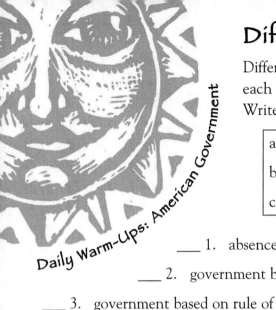

Different Types of Government

Different countries have different types of government. Match each type of government in the box with its description below. Write the correct letter on the line.

a. anarchy	d. dictatorship	f. monarchy
b. aristocracy	e. democracy	g. theocracy
c. communism		

___ 1. absence of government

___ 2. government based on religion or subject to religious authority

___ 3. government based on rule of the people

___ 4. government controlled by an absolute ruler

___ 5. government based on a hereditary ruling class or nobility

___ 6. government ruled by an individual with hereditary right to rule

___ 7. government ruled by an authoritarian party that controls the economy and aims to achieve a higher social order

163

Totalitarianism

It has been argued that totalitarianism violates essential human rights. The United States government has tended to oppose all forms of totalitarian rule.

In a few sentences, define totalitarianism. Explain why the United States opposes such governments.

164

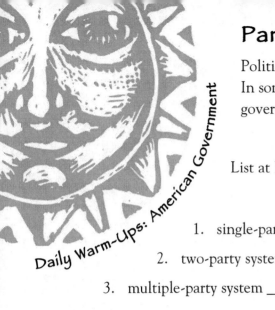

Parties in Government

Political parties play a role in the governments of many countries. In some countries, only one political party is involved in the government. In others, two or more parties are involved.

List at least two countries for each system below.

1. single-party system _____ _____

2. two-party system _____ _____

3. multiple-party system _____ _____

165

Working Together

The pairs of terms listed below all relate to political parties. The words in each pair either mean the same thing (synonyms), or have different meanings (antonyms). For each pair, say whether the words are antonyms or synonyms. Then define both terms.

1. a. plurality   b. minority

   _____

   _____

2. a. voting bloc   b. coalition

   _____

   _____

3. a. consensus   b. agreement

   _____

   _____

4. a. compromise   b. confrontation

   _____

   _____

166

Debate and Deliberation

Two approaches to talking about issues are debate and deliberation. Both approaches have things in common. But they are also different in many ways.

Think about debate and deliberation as they are used in politics. Consider the objectives of both approaches, and the processes they use. Think about the types of settings both are used in.

Now write a paragraph in which you compare and contrast debate and deliberation.

167

Market Economy (Capitalism)

The U.S. economic system is described as a mixed economy. However, it is based on the essential principles of capitalism, or a market economy.

The terms in the box refer to the capitalist system. Use them to answer the questions below. Write the appropriate term on the line.

competition	profit incentive
entrepreneurs	supply and demand

1. Who controls the means of production? _____

2. What is the motivation for production? _____

3. How is it determined what and how much should be produced?

    _____

4. What keeps product quality and prices reasonable?

    _____

Supply and Demand

Adam Smith wrote about economics in the 1700s. He believed that the forces behind supply and demand were like an invisible hand that kept an economy balanced.

Write a paragraph in which you explain the relationship between the quantity of goods a supplier is willing to make for a given profit, and the quantity of goods a consumer is willing to buy at a given price.

169

Command or Centrally Planned Economy (Socialism)

The command or centrally planned economy was a dominant feature of Communist countries. Most of these countries now have mixed economies. However, some retain strong command or socialist features.

The terms in the box refer to the command economy. Use them to answer the questions below. Write the appropriate term on the line.

central planning	need
common good	state

1. Who owns the means of production? _____

2. What is the motivation for production? _____

3. What is the basis for deciding what to produce, and how much to produce?

    _____

4. What is the role of government? _____

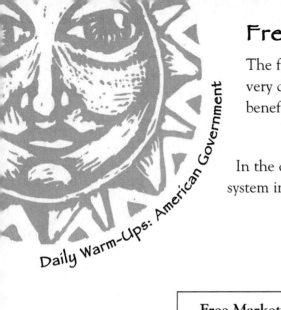

Free Market Versus Centrally Planned

The free market and centrally planned economic approaches are very different. Both claim to achieve the greatest economic benefits. However, both have benefits and drawbacks.

In the chart below, outline the benefits and drawbacks of each system in its pure form.

	Free Market Economy	Centrally Planned Economy
Benefits		
Drawbacks		

171

Government Intervention

In theory, capitalism may seem like an ideal system. In practice, it can lead to many problems. Among these are monopolies and trusts, poor working conditions, child labor, and product "dumping" by foreign countries.

Over the years, the U.S. government has become involved in the economy to benefit workers, entrepreneurs, and corporations. List as many ways you can think of that the government affects our mixed economy.

172

Outsourcing

As American companies expand and do business all over the globe, certain problems have arisen. One issue is outsourcing jobs—for example, transferring manufacturing jobs to workers overseas.

The rationale is that oursourcing enables companies to produce their goods for less. Workers in some countries accept lower wages than U.S. workers. Hiring these workers to produce goods helps the economy of the country where they live and work. However, it can also mean a loss of manufacturing jobs in the United States.

Do you think the U.S. government should act to stop companies from outsourcing manufacturing jobs? Why or why not? What action should it take? Write a paragraph for your answer.

173

Nationalized Health Care

Some argue that government should provide nationalized health care. In other words, the government should pay to make sure that all U.S. citizens have access to health care. Others say that such a program would go against the basic principles of our country.

Do you think nationalized health care is in accordance with U.S. values? Why or why not? Write a paragraph explaining your opinion.

174

Illegal Aliens

An **illegal alien** is a person who was born in another country but who now lives in the United States without government permission. It has been estimated that between 5 million and 8 million illegal immigrants live in the United States today. Write one or two sentences to answer each question below about illegal aliens.

1. Why are there so many illegal immigrants in the United States?

   _____

   _____

   _____

2. Should illegal aliens have the same right to due process that U.S. citizens have? Why or why not?

   _____

   _____

   _____

175

© 2006 Walch Publishing

Immigration

Immigrants from elsewhere founded the United States. Even today, immigration to the United States continues to affect the national identity.

The terms in the box have to do with immigration. Match each one with its description below. Write the correct letter on the line.

a. alien	c. deportation	e. immigrant
b. citizen	d. expatriation	f. naturalization

___ 1. a full member of the nation who owes allegiance to it and is entitled to all of the rights and privileges accorded to members

___ 2. a legal process by which noncitizens are removed from the country

___ 3. foreign-born or noncitizen resident

___ 4. a person who moves permanently to another country

___ 5. legal process by which a citizen is stripped of citizenship

___ 6. legal process by which a citizen of one country becomes a citizen of another

Foreign Aid

One of the most powerful foreign policy tools of the United States is its ability to provide or withhold aid to foreign countries. Foreign aid can take many forms. They include economic, humanitarian, and military support.

In 2004, these countries were among the top recipients of U.S. aid:

Afghanistan	Iraq	Liberia
Bolivia	Israel	Pakistan
Colombia	Jordan	Peru
Egypt	Kenya	Sudan

What does this list say about the interests of the United States? Write two or three sentences for your answer.

177

Cold War

The modern political world has been shaped, in great part, by the twentieth-century conflict known as the Cold War. Answer each question below about the Cold War.

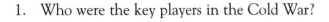

1. Who were the key players in the Cold War?

   _____

2. What was at issue during the Cold War? _____

   _____

   3. What was the arms race? _____

   _____

   4. What was the domino theory? _____

   _____

   5. How did the Cold War end? _____

   _____

178

NATO

One organization in which the United States is deeply invested is NATO. Answer the questions below about this organization.

1. What does the acronym NATO stand for?

   _____

   _____

2. Who are the major members of NATO?

   _____

   _____

3. Why was NATO formed?

   _____

   _____

179

The UN

Many issues involve more than one country. These issues range from depletion of rain forests to pollution to the threat of nuclear weapons. It is almost impossible for a country to function in complete isolation.

The UN is the major world forum for countries to work together. Answer the questions below about this organization.

1. What do the initials "UN" stand for? _____

2. When and why was the UN formed? _____

_____

_____

180

3. Do you believe the UN can be successful in securing world peace? Why or why not?

_____

_____

_____

1. Answers will vary, but should include reference to some form of organization that makes and enforces laws in society in order to protect against chaos or anarchy.

2. 1. b; 2. c; 3. a

3. 1. T; 2. F; It says a government should be abolished when it fails to protect natural rights. 3. T; 4. T; 5. F; The Bill of Rights is part of the U.S. Constitution.

4. 1. not able to be separated from; 2. Answers will vary, but might include reference to the vast amount of land available in the Americas that was not available in Britain.

5. Answers will vary. Sample answer: Pure Democracy—Strength: In theory, it allows every voice to be heard on every issue, leaving no one out; Weakness: Tyranny of the majority, an uneducated populace consumed by constant voting, and the cost and practicality of planning frequent votes. Republic—Strength: More coherent and efficient debate and voting; Weakness: Poor representation, districting that represses a particular perspective.

6. 1. Congress has the power to raise and maintain an army, a navy, and a national guard. 2. Congress has the power to impose taxes and borrow money. 3. States are denied the power to tax exports and imports, although Congress can tax imports. 4. Only Congress can coin money.

7. 1. The power of the government rests with the people and can exist only with the consent of the people. 2. Government is restricted in its power. 3. Citizens have rights and freedoms that are guaranteed and protected against government intrusion. 4. Power is divided and shared among different branches of government. 5. Different branches or parts of government "check" the activities of the other branches to ensure power is not being abused.

8. 1. F; Twelve states were represented; Rhode Island

refused to send a delegate to the convention. 2. F; Jefferson was serving as minister to France during the Convention, and the document itself was assembled by committee. 3. T; 4. F; The New Jersey plan called for equal representation among the states, while the Virginia or Madison plan proposed representation based on population. 5. T; 6. T; 7. F; Most delegates had served in government at some level; as a whole, the assembly had a great deal of political experience.

9. Confederation refers to a group of individual states that share power. Federation refers to a central government that has power over member states. In a confederation, consensus is difficult. In a federation, there is some loss of power in the states.

10. Answers will vary. Sample answers: 1. strengthen and improve the nation economically, socially, morally, and in terms of justice; 2. ensure fair application of the law; 3. ensure that people can live and function in a peaceful and orderly society; 4. protect against foreign threats; 5. provide for the needs and safety of citizens; 6. protect rights and freedoms for ourselves and future generations

11. 1. F; 2. S; 3. S; 4. F

12. 1. J; 2. L; 3. E; 4. L; 5. E; 6. L; 7. J

13. 1. C; 2. D; 3. R; 4. R; 5. D; 6. C

14. 1. F; Neither state nor national government can tax exports. 2. T; 3. F; Neither state nor national government can grant titles of nobility. 4. F; Only the national government can coin money. 5. T

15. Answers will vary. Sample answer: This clause makes it clear to the states that the federal system places national law above state law. It also protects all citizens against abuses by the states.

16. Alexander Hamilton

17. Answers will vary. Sample answers: The executive branch carries out the law. It checks the judicial branch by appointing judges to the Supreme Court. It checks the legislative branch by vetoing

legislation. The legislative branch makes laws. It checks the executive branch by overriding vetoes. It checks the judicial branch by approving or rejecting appointment of judges. The judicial branch interprets laws. It checks the executive branch by reviewing the constitutionality of executive orders. It checks the legislative branch by exerting judicial review over acts of Congress.

18. 1. T; 2. F; The Supreme Court has no power over constitutional amendments. 3. T; 4. T; 5. T; 6. F; The only restriction on constitutional amendments is that "no State, without its Consent, shall be deprived of its equal Suffrage in the Senate."

19. James Madison

20. 1. The national government would have a system of checks and balances. 2. There would be frequent elections and limitations on government. 3. The system of checks and balances and the lengthy process required for passing legislation

would prevent abuse. 4. The president would be regularly elected, could be impeached, and would be restricted in powers.

21. Answers will vary. Generally speaking, Madison's statements suggest that humans are, by nature, self-interested and power-hungry. As a result, the best way to keep government honest is to set up a system in which the ambition of one individual or group is controlled by the ambition of another individual or group.

22. 1. A faction is a united segment of the population, impassioned by a particular goal or interest that is adverse or potentially detrimental to another part of society. 2. Madison discusses the protection of rights of all citizens, as well as the diverse and competing interests in various parts of society and divisions of government. 3. It is arguable that the slave trade and the Red Scare are examples of factions empowered.

23. 1. Answers will vary depending on students'

interests and knowledge. 2. Answers will vary. Sample answers: giving money to a special interest group, writing letters to senators and representatives, publicizing the importance of the issue, running for office

24. Answers will vary. Sample answers: 1. Equality includes the right to fair treatment under law for all and the idea that no group or individual has superior rights in society. 2. Freedom involves the ability to speak, act, earn, own, and function without limitation. 3. Individualism stresses the notions of freedom as they apply to each member of society. 4. Capitalism is the economic philosophy that is characterized by entrepreneurship, profit motive, competition, and supply and demand. The latter three values implicitly contain the idea that government involvement in the lives of people should be limited.

25. 1. Answers will vary. Sample answers: family, friends, historic events, mass media, schools, political organizations, religion, socioeconomic status; 2. Answers will vary, but could include discussion of how many young people share the political values of their parents.

26. Answers will vary. Poll results can be skewed by poor or leading questions, an insufficient sample size, a nonrepresentative sample, limited attention to margin of error, and so forth.

27. Answers will vary, but may include the need for citizens to be able to process information about issues, to understand how government works in order to participate effectively, and to have a sense of appreciation and concern for the continued success of the state.

28. 1. Answers will vary. Sample answers: homeless shelters, libraries, Big Brothers Big Sisters, Meals on Wheels; 2. Answers will vary.

29. 1. F; Media includes non-news items as well. 2. T; 3. F; Not all media is news. 4. T; 5. F; They are

mostly free of government control.

30. 1. c; 2. b; 3. a; 4. d

31. 1. c; 2. b; 3. a; Note that even journalists have different interpretations of these terms.

32. Answers will vary, but students should address the fact that anonymity can help support "whistle-blowers" who might otherwise be fearful of stepping out.

33. Answers will vary.

34. 1. d; 2. b; 3. b

35. Answers will vary. Students should consider issues involving freedom of speech as well as protection from undue influence.

36. Answers will vary.

37. 1. c; 2. a; 3. d; 4. b

38. 1. using a famous person to promote a product; 2. attempting to connect with the reader or viewer; 3. suggesting that "everyone is doing it"; 4. putting down opposing people and views; 5. creating fear in the minds of readers or viewers

if they do not opt for a particular person, agenda, or item.

39. Answers will vary. Sample answers: Who is the author? Is he or she affiliated with a particular organization? Was the piece written for a purpose? Is evidence used to back up points? Is the evidence sound? Are there "leading" words, particularly adjectives that suggest a bias?

40. Answers will vary. Sample answers: political party, position, voting record, age, morality, family, religion, appearance.

41. 1. c; 2. c; 3. b; 4. a

42. 1. C; 2. L; 3. L; 4. C; 5. Answers will vary.

43. 1. b; 2. a; 3. b; 4. d; 5. c

44. Answers will vary, but generally, minor parties draw attention to a significant need that is not being met by one of the major parties.

45. Answers will vary. Sample answers: Republicans are associated with conservative values, particularly with regard to social issues, preference

for states' rights, and commitment to defense. Democrats tend to be more liberal, both socially and economically, favoring things such as social welfare programs and government regulation of business.

46. 1. F; The group of people who have the right to vote is the electorate. 2. T; 3. F; Only free males age twenty-one and over could vote. 4. T; 5. F; Women received the legal right to vote after African-American males. 6. F; The Thirteenth Amendment freed slaves, and the Fourteenth gave them the rights of citizens.

47. 1. e; 2. b; 3. c; 4. d; 5. f; 6. a

48. Answers will vary. Sample answers: name recognition, voting record, press coverage that comes with holding the position

49. 1. During the Vietnam War, many soldiers under the age of twenty-one were considered old enough to fight and die for their country, but were not old enough to vote. The voting age was lowered to address this discrepancy. 2. Answers will vary.

50. Answers will vary. Sample answers: lack of time, apathy, lack of knowledge, and a feeling that individual votes have no impact

51. Answers will vary. Sample answers: Pros: increased voter participation; Cons: possibility of viruses and skewed results

52. 1. b; 2. a; 3. d; 4. c

53. Answers will vary.

54. 1. A caucus is a physical meeting of voters to deliberate and "stand" for a candidate. 2. A primary election is a ballot-based election for nomination. 3. Answers will vary. Primary elections tend to achieve better voter turnout, while a caucus may get voters who are willing to spend time listening to arguments.

55. 1. Only party members can participate in a closed primary. 2. Members of all parties can participate in an open primary. 3. Answers will vary.

56. Answers will vary. Sample answer: If both political

parties support similar policies and goals, voters will not be very motivated to vote, and election results will not point the nation in a clear and distinct direction.

57. 1. T; 2. F; In the 2004 election, California had fifty-five electoral votes compared with Rhode Island's four electoral votes; 3. T; 4. T; 5. T; 6. F; It gives more influence to larger states, which have more electoral votses.

58. Answers will vary, although some consider the challenges presented to be positive attributes of the electoral college system.

59. 1. S; 2. H; 3. S; 4. H; 5. S; 6. H

60. 1. b; 2. a; 3.c; 4. California, New York, and Texas have the most seats. 5. A census is taken every ten years. 6. Answers will vary.

61. Answers will vary.

62. 1. The speaker of the House is selected by the members of the House. 2. The speaker presides over the House, interprets rules, puts motions to a vote, rules on questions of procedure, and so forth. 3. As of 2006, the speaker of the House is J. Dennis Hastert (R., IL).

63. 1. c; 2. d; 3. b

64. 1. The president of the Senate is the vice president of the United States. 2. serves as official moderator of the Senate, breaks tie votes; 3. elected by the Senate from the majority party; 4. presides over the Senate in the absence of the vice president

65. 1. H; 2. H; 3. S; 4. S; 5. S; 6. S

66. 1. b; 2. f; 3. e; 4. d; 5. a; 6. c

67. Answers will vary. Sample answers: Pros: Interest groups have time, knowledge, and inclination that legislators may not have. Cons: Particular interests may be promoted, with the general good demoted.

68. 1. T; 2. F; The bill does not become law. 3. F; The bill does not become law. 4. T; 5. F; A two-thirds vote of both the House and the Senate is required.

69. 1. T; 2. F; Both the House and the Senate have

standing committees. 3. F; Both the House and the Senate have a budget committee. 4. T; 5. T

70. Answers will vary.

71. 1. F; It is made up of members of the House and the Senate. 2. T; 3. T; 4. T; 5. F; They are chosen by members of the majority party. 6. F; The majority party gets a majority of the seats on each standing committee, but the minority party is well represented—it gets much more than one tenth of the seats.

72. Answers will vary, but should address the size of the House versus the size of the Senate and the nature of the Senate as the more deliberative body.

73. A filibuster is used by senators who may be part of a minority and seek to delay a vote. The filibuster can buy time to gain support for a particular position or to alter a bill. In a filibuster, minority senators monopolize the Senate floor with lengthy speeches plus time-killing motions, quorum calls,

and other delaying tactics.

74. Answers will vary. Sample answers: Advantages: experience of members, easy protocol for leadership selection; Disadvantages: lack of innovative leadership from newly elected members, discourages younger members

75. Answers will vary.

76. 1. c; 2. a; 3. b; 4. b; 5. c

77. 1. b; 2. d; 3. a; 4. f; 5. c; 6. e

78. State government: income tax, sales tax, corporate tax, gift tax; Township or city government: property tax, excise tax; National government: income tax, gift tax, inheritance tax, impost tax

79. 1. writ of habeas corpus; The Constitution says that this right cannot be suspended except when rebellion or invasion threaten public safety. 2. bill of attainder; The Constitution says that neither Congress nor the states can pass such a measure. 3. ex post facto law; The Constitution says that neither Congress nor state legislatures may pass

such laws.

80. 1. Copyrights and patents encourage creativity and innovation, and provide just reward for efforts. 2. Through regulation, the government has the authority to enforce protection. 3. Answers will vary, but should note the conflicting concerns of individual/corporate rights versus public welfare. 4. Answers will vary.

81. Answers will vary, but since drugs are transported across state lines, this opens interpretation of the Commerce Clause.

82. 1. Answers will vary. Sample answers: disaster, excessive credit, death of a family member. 2. Answers will vary, but might mention the protection of rights against creditors or circumstances beyond the control of an individual.

83. This clause prevents legislators and the president from taking advantage of their positions at the expense of taxpayers.

84. Answers will vary. Students should note that the clause allows for unforeseen needs, but that its interpretation is based in great part on philosophy of government.

85. 1. A revenue bill focuses on methods for raising money, such as taxes and tariffs. 2. a. 7; b. 4; c. 1; d. 6; e. 2; f. 5; g. 3. Note: Bills of revenue must originate in the House.

86. Answers as of mid-2006: 1. George W. Bush; 2. Dick Cheney; 3. Condoleezza Rice; 4. Donald Rumsfeld; 5. Stephen Hadley; 6. Michael Chertoff; 7. Alberto Gonzales; 8. Joshua Bolton

87. 1. b; 2. c; 3. d; 4. d

88. Answers will vary, but may include being Christian, having no legal convictions, being male, and having experience.

89. 1. The Twenty-second Amendment was passed primarily in response to the expansion of presidential power under Franklin D. Roosevelt; 2. Limiting the presidential term prevents an excess of power and offers others the opportunity

to lead; 3. Answers will vary.

90. 1. The qualifications for vice president are the same as for president; 2. to serve as president of the Senate and to break tie votes in that body, and to assume the presidency if called upon to do so; 3. The president makes an appointment that must be approved by a majority of both the House and the Senate.

91. 1. Generally, "balancing the ticket" means finding a candidate for vice president who is from a different part of the country and might be favored by another demographic group of society.
2. Answers will vary. Sample answer: A Catholic female from the Midwest, the daughter of a navy pilot, who went to the University of Chicago and now lives in Pennsylvania.

92. Answers will vary. Sample answer: The system protects against a vice presidential usurpation of power and ensures that action can be taken even if the president is not making sound decisions.

93. The order of succession places power first in the hands of elected officials who already have extensive power and experience in government. The first four Cabinet members arguably protect the most essential interests of our country and thus have the most power. The other heads of the Cabinet are listed in the order in which the offices were created by Congress.

94. 1. the House of Representatives; 2. a majority vote; 3. the Senate; 4. a two-thirds vote; 5. removal from office and prohibition from the benefits of office, although individuals can still be tried in regular court

95. The president is the main force behind the nation's public policies. The president initiates and suggests legislation and requests and sometimes demands that Congress enact it.

96. 1. e; 2. b; 3. a; 4. f; 5. c; 6. d

97. 1. T; 2. F; The ordinance power is clearly intended in the Constitution. 3. T; 4. F; The president can

authorize subordinates to issue executive orders.

98. 1. A veto is the presidential power to officially reject a bill passed by Congress (which must occur within ten days of receipt of a bill, or the bill automatically passes). 2. A pocket veto occurs when Congress adjourns within ten days of submitting a bill and the president does not sign or reject a bill within the time allowed to do so. 3. A pocket veto means that since Congress is not in session, it cannot override a veto. (There has been some debate over the length of adjournment necessary for a pocket veto to apply.)

99. A line-item veto might allow a spending bill to be passed much more quickly, with less deliberation. An argument against the line-item veto is that the president might gain too much power over spending with this ability.

100. 1. to put together a working budget, 2. all White House offices, departments, and independent agencies; 3. prioritizing goals, approving the budget, and submitting it to Congress for approval; 4. This can happen if less revenue is taken in than in the previous year.

101. 1. c; 2. d; 3. e; 4. b; 5. a; 6. g; 7. f

102. Answers will vary. Sample answers: War, recession, and natural disaster are all situations in which deficit spending may be acceptable.

103. 1. e; 2. f; 3. a; 4. d; 5.c; 6. b

104. 1. Y; 2. N; elected by House members; 3. Y; 4. Y; 5. N; elected by Senate members; 6. N; elected or appointed in state; 7. Y; 8. Y

105. 1. b; 2. a; 3. c; 4. a; 5. b; 6. b

106. 1. b; 2. c; 3. a; 4. d; 5. Answers will vary.

107. Answers will vary, but should address the concepts of undue influence on government and abuse of position.

108. 1. suggestive of an emperor, controlling; 2. Yes; the term implies that the president has too much power and acts without the proper approval from Congress. 3. Answers will vary, but may address

the expansion of White House offices and the increased number of personal advisors as well as the extension of power through executive directives and agreements.

109. Answers will vary. Sample answers: 1. freedom from obligations, less likelihood of becoming involved in conflicts between other nations; 2. may decline to intervene in situations where intervention could save many lives (e.g., genocide, famine); may lose the benefit of alliances that provide economic or security benefits; may not have allies in case of invasion; 3. Answers will vary.

110. Answers will vary. Sample answers: 1. can affect the outcome of events in a desirable manner, can prevent human rights abuses, can protect important resources; 2. can be costly in troops or supplies, can make enemies; 3. to protect against human rights abuses

111. 1. An executive agreement is a binding legal agreement between the president and another head of state that does not require Senate approval. 2. A treaty is a formal agreement between the United States and another country that requires Senate approval. 3. the president; 4. the president or envoys; 5. the president; 6. the Senate

112. 1. Congress can declare war, raise/oversee armed forces, fund missions, make rules of war, and call up militia. 2. Answers will vary. Sample answer: The War Powers Resolution was a response to the war in Vietnam. It was intended to limit the president's power regarding war.

113. 1. conducts diplomatic relations with other countries, maintains embassies, advises the president; 2. controls the U.S. military, advises the president; 3. collects and analyzes intelligence information, advises the president; 4. ensures the readiness of the various armed forces, advises the president

114. Ambassadors advise and protect American citizens in foreign countries. They issue visas to foreign citizens for travel to the United States. They provide information to foreign governments about the concerns and policies of the United States. They also negotiate, resolve conflicts, and provide aid to other countries.

115. Answers will vary, but may include discussion of the diverse laws, cultures, and customs that a diplomat may inadvertently violate. The practice also protects privacy and acknowledges the diplomatic objective of fostering positive relations.

116. Answers will vary. Sample answers: 1. Army: responsible for ground-based military operations; 2. Navy: responsible for sea-based military operations; 3. Air Force: responsible for air-based military operations. Other forces: Coast Guard, Marines.

117. Answers will vary. Sample answers: Benefits: appreciation for civilian concerns, awareness of diplomatic options; Negatives: lack of experience to make accurate judgments, insufficient appreciation for what is involved in military ventures

118. Answers will vary.

119. 1. There are nine judges on the Supreme Court. 2. There is no age requirement. 3. There is none specified. 4. Answers will vary.

120. Answers as of mid-2006: 1. Chief Justice John Roberts; 2. John Paul Stevens, Antonin Scalia, Anthony Kennedy, David Souter, Clarence Thomas, Ruth Bader Ginsburg, Stephen Breyer, Samuel Alito

121. Answers will vary. Sample answer: Being appointed for life means that federal judges are unlikely to be subject to outside influences and can base their decisions solely on the law and their interpretation of it. If they were elected, they might be vulnerable to the desires of their constituents. If they were appointed for a set term,

such as four years, with reappointment depending on the executive or legislative branch, they might be swayed by their desire to be reappointed. The lifetime appointment preserves the justices from such influences.

122. 1. the power of a court to hear a case first, before any other court; 2. the authority of a court to review lower, or inferior, court decisions; 3. appellate; 4. cases involving foreign diplomats or states

123. Answers will vary. Sample answer: Judicial review is the ability of the court to determine whether state and federal laws, acts of Congress, and executive orders are constitutional.

124. 1. returned; 2. request by a lower court, when that court is not certain about procedure or rule of law, to certify an answer to a specific question; 3. an order by the Supreme Court to have the lower court send up a record of a particular case

125. 1. briefs from "friends of the court," or briefs written by third parties who have an interest in the case and can offer unique or expanded insights; 2. rulings, decisions on cases with rationale to support them; 3. a decision that stands as an example to be followed in future cases and that is binding in state and federal courts

126. 1. The majority opinion announces the Court's decision in a case and gives the reasoning it is based on. 2. A concurring opinion is written in addition to a majority opinion by a justice or justices who wish to stress a different or additional rationale for the decision. 3. A dissenting opinion is written by a justice or justices who disagree with the Court's majority opinion.

127. 1. L; 2. R; 3. L; 4. R; 5. L

128. 1. the first ten amendments to the U.S. Constitution; 2. in the Constitution; 3. They include freedoms of speech, press, assembly, petition, and religious practice; the right to bear arms; protections against search and seizure;

guarantees of due process; and protection of states' rights.

129. 1. These laws restricted the rights of African Americans, named after a minstrel-show character that stereotyped African Americans as being dim-witted and clumsy. 2. Separate facilities for Americans of European and African descent (effectively separating the races) was not a violation of the civil rights of African Americans so long as facilities existed for both groups. 3. segregation by legal code; 4. segregation not by law but in practice (note to students that de facto segregation still exists)

130. 1. b; 2. d; 3. a; 4. c

131. 1. a fee for voting; many African Americans could not afford to pay the fee; 2. tests of ability to read and write; in some areas, different tests were given to white and black voters, with black voters receiving more difficult tests; in other areas, "grandfather clauses" allowed voting to anyone who could vote before 1870, or the descendants of anyone who could vote before 1870, regardless of literacy; this effectively ruled out African Americans while allowing illiterate whites to vote; 3. redrawing voting districts to give special advantages to one group; this was used to limit the effectiveness of black voters; 4. primary elections in which only white citizens could select candidates

132. 1. Thirteenth; 2. Twenty-fourth; 3. Fourteenth; 4. Fifteenth

133. Answers will vary, but may touch upon racism, limitations on credential-building opportunities, and the limited ability of government to impact wage practices of nonpublic entities.

134. Answers will vary, but may touch upon the need to equalize the playing field, or possibly the importance of holding to strict constitutional value on freedom from government interference in the lives of individuals.

135. 1. false or malicious use of the written word;
2. false or malicious use of the spoken word;
3. encouraging the violent or unlawful overthrow of the government

136. Answers will vary, but will likely touch on the subjectivity of determining literary or artistic "value" and who constitutes the "average" person.

137. Answers will vary.

138. 1. a formal request; 2. in order to form coalitions, share ideas, act freely; 3. the right to interact with whomever one chooses; 4. People have the right to assemble with whomever they wish. There can be no guilt by association.

139. Answers will vary, but should include reference to Miranda rights, having a public attorney provided if requested, presentation of charges, speedy trial, and presumption of innocence.

140. 1. f; 2. c; 3. d; 4. e; 5. a; 6. b

141. Answers will vary, but may look at the constitutional notion of promoting general welfare as opposed to the individual's right to property.

142. Answers will vary, but student paragraphs should acknowledge that giving up rights in one area may threaten rights in another.

143. 1. 50; 2. 48; 3. Hawaii, Alaska; 4. Article IV, Section 3 of the U.S. Constitution states that new states can be added with consent from Congress. 5. Answers will vary. Sample answer: Puerto Rico, Guam, other U.S. territories

144. Answers will vary.

145. Answers will vary. Sample answers: 1. Interstate compacts are mutual agreements to work together on a particular endeavor, including public university fee agreements and joint land preservation. 2. Extradition involves the return of an accused criminal to the state in which the crime was committed.

146. 1. T; 2. F; According to the Full Faith and Credit Clause, the laws of Texas apply in Texas, so the driver cannot drive according to the Louisiana

speed limit. 3. T; 4. F; The Illinois legal system would be obliged to extradite the accused person to North Dakota so that the state whose laws were broken could try the person.

147. 1. b; preschool programs, forest preservation; 2. c; scientific research, arts development, scholarships; 3. a; education, welfare, transportation

148. Answers will vary. Sample answer: Generally speaking, states think they know what they need better than the federal government and can use funds more appropriately where they are needed within the state. Federal officials see the expenditure of taxpayer dollars on unknown programs that vary from region to region as a recipe for misallocation. Some believed that if there was a surplus of funds it should be returned to taxpayers within the states and sought as revenue by state governments. Others argue that times of deficit are not times for revenue sharing.

149. 1. A referendum involves citizens voting directly on issues. Bond issues are often presented in a referendum. 2. A citizen's initiative allows citizens to force a public vote on an issue by having a petition signed by a certain minimum number of registered voters.

150. Answers will vary, but may focus on recall as an extension of democracy and another check on government offset by potential abuse by an erratic public.

151. 1. F; 2. S; 3. F; 4. F; 5. F; 6. S

152. 1. f; 2. d; 3. e; 4. c; 5. a; 6. b

153. 1. f; 2. d; 3. a; 4. c; 5. b; 6. e

154. Answers will vary. Sample answer: A good jury is one whose members are open-minded, are not influenced by bias, are committed to following the law, believe in the principle that the accused is innocent until proven guilty, reflect the makeup of the general population in both gender and ethnicity, and are willing to comply with court rules about confidentiality.

155. Answers will vary, but may touch upon the different rules and codes of conduct for military personnel, and different expectations in combat situations, balanced by a nonmilitary appeals process to ensure no military abuse of power.

156. 1. The governor appoints and removes state officials and members of the judiciary, supervises departments, proposes budgets, offers clemency, oversees state national guard, calls special sessions, and promotes legislative agenda. 2. The lieutenant governor presides over the state senate and succeeds the governor if necessary. 3. The secretary of state records acts of government and administers election laws. 4. The treasurer controls state tax collection, budget, and payroll. 5. The attorney general serves as legal advisor to the governor and to departments of the state.

157. 1. T; 2. F; Each state sets the formal qualifications for its governor. 3. T; 4. T; 5. T; 6. F; As in the federal legislature, a bill can be introduced in either house.

158. 1. b; 2. c; 3. d; 4. a

159. 1. b; 2. d; 3. c; 4. a; 5. e

160. Answers will vary. Sample answers: Advantages—the community supports the education of its young citizens; students of all socioeconomic levels get a free and equal public education. Disadvantages—people with no school-age children have to help pay for education; property taxes may become very high, with lower-income citizens unable to pay; economy-minded citizens may underfund public education to keep property taxes down.

161. 1. a; 2. c; 3. d; 4. b

162. Answers will vary, but should include defined state boundaries, independent from control of any other country, represented by a distinct government.

163. 1. a; 2. g; 3. e; 4. d; 5. b; 6. f; 7. c

164. Answers will vary. Sample answer: Totalitarianism involves the political entity (of whatever type) controlling all aspects of human activity, which

would minimize basic rights of speech, property ownership, and so forth. Since the United States holds that these rights are fundamental human rights, it opposes governments that seek to withhold these rights from their citizens.

165. Answers will vary. Sample answers: 1. single-party system: China, Cuba, North Korea; 2. two-party system: United States, Canada, Britain; 3. multiple-party system: Israel, Italy

166. 1. antonyms; a. the largest share of something, which may or not be a majority; in an election with three candidates, one of whom received 45% of the vote while the others received 20% and 35%, the candidate with 45% of the vote would win with a plurality, but would not have a majority, or more than half, of the votes; b. a group that has less than the number of votes needed for control; 2. synonyms, both suggesting a temporary alliance; a. a group of legislators who act together for some common purpose; b. a

temporary alliance of political parties; in some political systems, when no one party receives a majority of the votes, two or more of the minority parties will form a coalition government; 3. synonyms; a. group solidarity of opinion; b. an arrangement as to a course of action; 4. antonyms; a. a settling of differences in which each side makes concessions; b. a face-to-face disagreement brought about by clashing ideas or opinions

167. Answers will vary. Sample answer: Debate is often used by opposing candidates as a forum for highlighting their strengths in relation to their opponent. In debate, both parties highlight opposing views and try to win points over each other. Debate can involve attacking one's opponent's opinions and actions. Deliberation is a decision-making process where all parties work to consider all sides of an issue and come to an agreement on a course of action.

168. 1. entrepreneurs; 2. profit incentive; 3. supply and

demand; 4. competition

169. Answers will vary. Sample answer: The greater the profit margin, the more goods a supplier will be willing to make. Consumers will buy more product as the price decreases. Where these two intersect is the optimal production for greatest profit for supplier and best price for quantity for the consumer.

170. 1. state; 2. common good; 3. need; 4. central planners

171. Answers will vary. Sample answers: Free Market Economy: Benefits—offers great rewards for success; Drawbacks—offers no protection to the worker; did not predict the problem of monopoly. Centrally Planned Economy: Benefits—takes care of citizens, prevents homelessness; Drawbacks—producers less motivated to produce, innovate, develop new products or methods.

172. Answers will vary. Sample answers: trust regulation, minimum wage, subsidy, tariffs, safety standards

173. Answers will vary.

174. Answers will vary.

175. Answers will vary. Sample answers for #1 might include the desire for a better life economically and materially, and the very long wait for approval for legal immigration.

176. 1. b; 2. c; 3. a; 4. e; 5. d; 6. f

177. Answers will vary. Sample answer: U.S. foreign policy concerns span the globe, and a variety of different nations are targeted for foreign aid for a variety of reasons—for example, Israel to ensure its continued existence and Sudan for humanitarian purposes and Columbia to help fight the war on drugs.

178. 1. United States, Soviet Union; 2. communism versus capitalism; 3. competition for nuclear dominance; 4. fear that countries could fall, one by one, to communism; 5. Soviet policies of *glasnost* and *perestroika*, the collapse of the Soviet Union, and gradual introduction of free-market

practices simultaneous to elections for government positions

179. 1. North Atlantic Treaty Organization;
2. European countries and the United States;
3. NATO was designed to defend against communism during the Cold War.

180. 1. United Nations; 2. The UN was formed after World War II to prevent another global conflict and to protect human rights against such a genocide as occurred during that conflict.
3. Answers will vary.

Turn downtime into learning time!

For information on other titles in the

Daily *Warm-Ups* series,

visit our web site: walch.com